THE SCIENCE OF TALENT

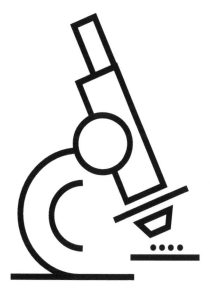

HOW TO FIND, GROW AND KEEP THE RIGHT PEOPLE IN YOUR ORGANISATION

KATE O'LOUGHLIN

The Science of Talent

First published in 2018 by

Panoma Press Ltd
48 St Vincent Drive, St Albans, Herts, AL1 5SJ, UK
info@panomapress.com
www.panomapress.com

Book layout by Neil Coe.

Printed on acid-free paper from managed forests.

ISBN 978-1-784521-25-7

This book is available online and in bookstores.

DEDICATION

For Dad, who taught me everything I know about business, and for Chris, whose patience and love have kept me going.

TESTIMONIALS

This is a great book. It has challenged my thinking and provoked me to think differently about talent management. I've taken away things that I can implement straight away whilst also giving me plenty of food for thought for longer-term improvements.

Dan Hardaker, Head of HR, Heineken UK

Clear, concise, easy to read and comprehensive coverage of the subject. This book offers a nice balance of knowledge of the subject, review of the literature and research which is particularly helpful for someone working broadly in this space. It constantly challenges the validity of talent programmes and processes. A very useful and insightful book.

Adrienne Gault, Head of People, Transformation and Organisational Change, Food Standards Agency

Kate is a true expert in her field, she's passionate, engaging and a joy to work with.

Jennifer Heyes, Head of Talent and Development, Vodafone UK

There are quite a few books covering talent management, but this is the first that I've found easy and interesting to read from cover to cover. It's low on jargon (and where it is introduced it is always explained) and it's very practical and no-nonsense in its approach. Peppered with real examples it is inspiring... no more time to write this review I need to start making some changes!

Ted Smith, Director of People & Places, Wellcome Trust

ACKNOWLEDGEMENTS

Thank you to my fabulous coach, Mindy Gibbins-Klein, and the book group who encouraged me to keep going, Elva, Karen, Mary, Angela, Hazel and Justyn.

To my wonderful test readers and those who gave me feedback on early drafts, thank you for your attention to detail and helpful suggestions: Ted Smith, Jenni Heyes, Shan Martin, Ginny Smith, Ian Dabson, Dan Hardaker, Wayne Palmer, Adi Gault and Sarah Malone.

CONTENTS

Testimonials		4
Acknowledgements		6
Chapter 1	Introduction	9
Chapter 2	Why it matters	13
Chapter 3	What is talent?	27
Chapter 4	Working out what you need	39
Chapter 5	Finding talent	53
Chapter 6	Promoting talent	63
Chapter 7	Measuring talent	77
Chapter 8	Growing talent	89
Chapter 9	Keeping talent	107
Chapter 10	Replacing talent	121
Chapter 11	Leadership	127
Chapter 12	Conclusion	141
Appendix		147
Endnote references		149
About the Author		157

CHAPTER 1

INTRODUCTION

When I was a little girl my favourite word was 'Why?' closely followed by 'Who?', 'What?', 'Where?' and 'When?' I must have driven mum and dad mad asking the same questions over and over again. My curiosity was insatiable. I was always thinking about why things happened in a particular way. As I grew up, I realised that sometimes the hardest question to answer is 'How?' How could things be improved if they were done a different way? What would happen if nothing changed? This book is for people like me who are curious to understand how things work and why sometimes they don't, even though they should. What are the facts? I will be asking questions and challenging some assumptions that we have all made about 'Talent' and suggesting some ways in which the definition of talent might need to change. I don't pretend to have all of the answers, but by asking the questions, I hope you might question what you are doing and perhaps make a few changes.

Lots of people know that 'talent happens' in their organisation, but many are not quite sure what 'talent' is or how 'it' happens. So much of what is done is behind closed doors, sometimes for good reasons, sometimes not. But this means that it can be difficult for anyone who wants to know more to really understand what is done and why it is done in a particular way.

I spent most of my early working life in large and medium-sized corporates before setting up my own business as an independent HR Consultant and Executive Coach, working with businesses of all sizes and shapes. My work with clients has given me a different perspective but it has never stopped me asking: 'Why do we do it that way?' 'Is that still relevant?' 'What needs to change?'

This book will consider what worked and what didn't work in practice, and then look at how things are changing. It will look at what current research evidence is telling us and why things may still need to change. More importantly, it will provide some ideas on how to make change happen in practical ways that will generate a stronger return on investment.

There is currently a great deal in the popular press about how to deal with managing people in the new economy: ideas that span getting rid of appraisals through to managing diversity and millennials differently. In this book I will be taking a look at what the science tells us about the theory behind these ideas and whether making some of the changes being suggested are a good idea or not. This book will help anyone looking to make changes to really think through why the change needs to happen and give some practical advice about how that might be done.

It can be used as a general guide for Managers and HR teams who have an interest or a need to find, grow and keep the right people in their organisations, so that they can be successful. It creates a structure to review current practice and figure out whether what has been done to date is still fit for purpose.

Books have been written about each aspect of what we call the 'talent pipeline' – what we mean by that is how a business recruits, develops and retains its people – but few have revisited the new reality of what is happening in the world as it changes from a holistic perspective. Many of these books are extremely useful and I would urge readers to read any that are of particular interest. This book is different, in that it covers an overview of all of the different talent activities, with an insight into the evidence underpinning the practice, accompanied by real life examples of where this has succeeded, or failed, in different settings. The examples have been drawn from a wide variety of organisations. The importance of these examples is not whether they are like your own company or not, but what you can learn from what happened. The intention is for the reader to consider what they would take or leave from each chapter and how that might be applied. To help with this, each chapter has a summary outlining top tips. These can be used as a reminder or a shorthand review of the chapter.

This book is not intended to be a comprehensive review of all talent initiatives in every company. Rather, it is a collection of current thinking about how organisations adopt and apply 'talent' practices. It is based on real life examples and is a moment in time. It does not pretend to provide answers to all the questions, but it does put them together into one place so that organisations can take an overview of the area and make some decisions about how to do what they need to do.

For those who have no idea what talent is but have heard the term, talent is generally about highlighting those people in organisations who have potential to go further. For those who already have a talent initiative in their organisation, you might like to consider taking a short questionnaire both before and after reading this book to see whether your views have changed (see Appendix). Most organisations apply the term to leadership roles only, but those that do miss the really critical people who may be key to their organisation's future success. This book examines why and how to 'do' talent, drawing on best practice and theory. It doesn't attempt to give a standard definition of what talent is, but provides some tools and practices for organisations to define that for themselves. Some organisations apply a politically correct lens to the label and call all the people in their organisation talent. Indeed they are, but this misses the point. Essentially talent is a form of risk management. If you want to stay in business and be successful – growing, changing shape, even downsizing – then you need to ensure that you give yourself the best chance of success. That means being able to identify the people that will make the biggest difference, and understanding what you need to do to succeed in finding, growing and keeping them.

CHAPTER 2

WHY IT MATTERS

During its strategic planning sessions, the board of directors of a major FTSE 100 organisation agreed that it needed to grow new territory and defend current market share. As a result they decided to expand on the South Coast and had planned a huge marketing campaign to do so, at great expense, before consulting the talent team. It was only at the point that the team was brought in that it became clear that full employment on the South Coast meant that recruitment of the necessary technical staff was going to be highly complicated, time consuming and costly. The talent team began to review demographic data and to 'market map' how much the resource would cost to bring in from Europe. The only country capable of providing sufficient numbers of technical staff was Poland. So the team began to crunch the numbers and do some 'heat mapping', only to discover that recruiting the people they needed to execute the work escalated the cost of the strategy beyond its economic worth. A second plan was developed to train people in sufficient numbers to do the job, but given the rate of pay, length of time it would take to train someone, and lack of recruits due to the low levels of unemployment it became clear that it was impossible, and the expansion plans, along with the very expensive marketing campaign, had to be abandoned.

Surprisingly, examples such as this may not be very common, but they are not the exception either. As this so-called VUCA (volatile, uncertain, complex, ambiguous) world is changing, companies continue to wage the 'war for talent' to get ahead of the competition. But it is questionable whether today's talent practices – how you find (talent acquisition), grow (talent development) and keep (talent retention) the right people in an organisation – have kept up with those changes.

Getting it right

Where talent is properly embedded and taken seriously by senior leaders as a critical tool for them to use to grow and shape their business, it can have a very positive impact.

Example:

A FTSE 100 blue chip organisation benefited from a share price rise of four points when an internal candidate was appointed as the next CEO. Much was made in the press of the talent processes in this particular company being highly effective and well developed for leaders. This gave shareholders and the City confidence that the business was being well run by forward-thinking leaders who had anticipated and planned for the future. The business benefited and the talent function was applauded for its capability to impact the bottom line. It often does so, but not always in quite such an obvious way.

The so called 'gig economy' is throwing into question our understanding of how a business model operates and that has posed some serious questions about how employees and therefore 'talent' should be perceived and managed in the future. There is a rise in the number of organisations that have developed an 'outsourced' approach, i.e. the people who work there are not employed directly by the company as an employee, but instead are offered a contract for services. Entire businesses, such as the taxi firm Uber, were set up on the premise that their employees were independent contractors, not employees. In October 2016, Uber drivers successfully challenged their employment status in the courts. Similarly a group of couriers for the food takeaway delivery service, Deliveroo, have started taking legal steps to gain union recognition and workers' rights. More are following in their footsteps. This throws into question who is an employee, and where should consideration of 'talent' begin and end?

Other businesses have attempted different models in which they employ directly those people who are core to their capability as a business, and it is this which sets them apart from the competition whilst attempting to contain costs through having a peripheral workforce or 'non-core' workers, labelled by researchers as 'boundaryless'[1]. These non-employed workers move between and within firms, or even professions, managing their own careers, rather than the organisation doing it for them. Those who fall into this category have been labelled as having 'protean careers'[2]. Those who follow a protean career path may move between periods of focus on work and non-work priorities, according to their own values, wants and needs. So what does this mean for the talent agenda? Who can be considered to be 'in' an organisation? How should businesses treat this conundrum to ensure that they get the best from their people and their people get the best from them, when they are not sure who "their people" are?

At a practical level, how should you go about attracting, motivating and retaining workers in a heterogeneous workforce who may be pursuing traditional and non-standard career paths at different times in their careers? Most large employers have been able to rise to the challenge and are able to cater for both. Employment legislation has increasingly strengthened individual choice, e.g. part-time workers directive, parental leave legislation, etc, pushing businesses still further to deliver on a new business model. The introduction of flexible working has staved off the need for employees to leave a business in order to pursue their own interests, but this might be changing. As recently as May 2017 pioneers of telecommuting such as IBM, as well as many others, have recognised that the benefit of such working practices is weighted in favour of employees rather than employers and have announced an end to telecommuting[3]. Instead workers must now attend an office during working hours. This might well drive an increase in the number of people who choose to pursue independence in their work. This individual choice will, to a certain extent, be shaped by organisational forces, e.g. social norms and market pressures, but what we see is a complex interaction between the two, where both need to be involved and dependent on each other and yet wish to be separate.

What can organisations actually do, therefore, to facilitate the different demands placed on them by changing their own business models to contain costs and balance this with the talent agenda? We know what organisations want – to have the best people possible for their business – but what is not at all clear is what people really want. In their chapter on the changing world of work, Guest et al 2007 [4] refer to various studies that have sought to determine what people want from work. Unsurprisingly perhaps, the conclusion would appear to be that it depends on the individual and this means a myriad of solutions may be needed. Organisations will need to represent themselves in the recruitment market place as providing the opportunity for both traditional and non-standard career paths in a huge variety of different ways. This makes it incredibly difficult for employers to deliver a strong message about the advantages of being employees of that organisation, to appeal to individuals, not a mass market. This creates an interesting dynamic for the business that is seeking to find, develop and retain talent. Because it might be that the talent they seek does not want to be a part of their business unless certain conditions are met. Or that the talented individual wants to be part of their organisation, but this does not fit with their business model. Or that they want to be part of it sometimes, but not always. Talent plans for the business will have to evolve to encompass those outside the boundaries of the business without making them a part of the business. Throughout this book this will be a consideration for each aspect of talent.

Why have so many talent programmes failed in the past?

Despite the evidence of the first example in this book, in which the share price rose as a result of the CEO being internally appointed, most talent programmes, more specifically senior hiring, leadership development programmes and talent processes, are not perceived to be delivering. Dozens of articles have been written that demonstrate that in the opinion of senior managers, these programmes are failing to deliver on return on investment (ROI). Critics look to cast the blame at high profile programmes because that is where the 'cost' is most obvious and the expectation is greatest. Undoubtedly, some of these programmes are ill–conceived and may not have been well applied, leaving the business with a huge bill and not many promotable leaders as a result. However, in many instances it is because the talent acquisition, talent development programmes and talent processes are not fully aligned and are not as embedded in the corporate strategy and planning process as they need to be in order to make them effective.

In companies where the three elements of acquisition, development and retention are joined together, and are treated as part of the strategic planning process as equal partners and measured as any other serious risk to the business, there is much less likelihood that they will fail. However, companies frequently decide that they will make a senior appointment, launch a development programme or plan for talent separately. This leads to confusion and inefficiency. HR may be asked to recruit, develop and run the talent evaluation process, but may do so through entirely separate teams. Information is lost and the power for decisions about the process is devolved, rather than owned, by the Board, more specifically the CEO. As a result you may have the wrong people joining the business. They may do a great job but do not have the capability to become successors to more senior roles, they may then be invited to attend a high profile development programme and then fail to apply their learning back in the work place. At the next talent review round they are down-graded as a likely successor, and when they are told this they leave the business. Or worse still, they stay and block an opportunity because they have no other options. The business has lost a valuable opportunity to manage risk and blames the hiring process, the leadership development programme or the talent processes because they are such obvious targets.

So what types of things go wrong? Here are some examples of what could go wrong and then some real life examples of how those issues might be fixed.

1. Problem #1. Failure to plan for the future. Attrition of senior hires rises as appointments are made of those who may fit the bill at that point in time and then leave the business because they are ambitious and nobody thought through the implications of them joining. Generally a hiring manager will consider the current vacancy, and it will be well understood where the individual will fit now. But where will they go next? Constant churn at this level will have a significant impact on share price, morale and performance of a business.

Example:

Senior leadership attrition was running at 98%, due to a lack of planning and consideration of the candidates wishes for the future. Absence of a leadership framework meant that hires were being made randomly and the organisational 'fit' or 'future needs' of the business were not being considered. Candidates would join and then leave after a 12 month period as it became clear that the opportunity for them to progress was non-existent. This churn was destabilising the business. By introducing a leadership framework and development planning that revolved around succession discussions, attrition dropped to 25%, a far more manageable level. Still too high, but a marked improvement on what had been happening.

2. Problem #2. Failure to identify talent programme goals. Leadership development programmes are developed at great expense and swathes of managers may attend in sheep dip format but nothing changes. Nobody feels special because the programme is open to everyone. Nothing changes because the intention of the programme is unclear and it is discredited by those who attend because they don't know what is expected to change. Returning to the workplace and trying to make change happen is difficult because the business is resistant to the change that needs to be made.

Example:

A graduate scheme was introduced by a business, lots of delegates were attracted to join, but after many interviews very few people were hired because the leaders were competing for candidates. They had failed to see the purpose of the programme. The programme was considered to be a failure as no-one from the programme made it to the succession plans because that had never been the express intention. The programme fizzled out and the business believed that it was not possible to run a graduate programme.

However, one part of the business introduced a different graduate scheme that was intentionally introduced as a 'feeder' route for succession. It was based on calculations that suggested that 12 middle managers would be able to leave the business every year for the next six years due to the option to retire. This programme was a 'fix' for the perceived shortfall in candidates internally. But it sought to provide only 1/3 of the possible candidates for the positions becoming vacant. The reason was that there should be one candidate from outside the business, one from a different part of the business and one of the planned succession hires. The intention of the programme was very clear: it was there to fix a strategic problem. The CEO of this part of the business 'owned' the programme and led it very visibly. He made it clear what he expected not only of the delegates, but also of the business teams who would be welcoming the new recruits into their teams – a real job, with real responsibility. The talent programme was centrally run, and initially salaries, as well as development costs, were held in a central budget. Salaries were later devolved to the business as it became clear that the benefit of having such a delegate in a departmental team was worth the cost. The programme was seen as successful right the way across the business because it delivered candidates for more senior roles, as was the original intention, and a potential risk to the business in talent shortfall was averted by the implementation of a long-term plan.

3. Problem #3. Failure to analyse the data. Huge amounts of time and money are wasted on gathering data about talent and

risk that is reviewed by senior leaders once a year and then forgotten about, or disregarded, until a critical moment. The information is barely considered or challenged. It is simply a very labour intensive exercise that most people dread. Then, when it is actually expected to deliver the goods and highlight a future successor, it fails to do so. This happens because it is regarded as a tick box exercise that nobody ever believes will actually be used, so they are not totally open about the delegates. This is a waste of time and money for all concerned. It is probably better to not review talent at all than to waste everyone's time doing it as a tick box exercise. This self-deception creates an illusion of having things thought through and creates a false sense of security. At least those companies that do not run talent reviews know that they have not done it and so do not fall into the trap of being unprepared by doing half a job, as outlined in the example below:

Example:

A senior role became available and the identified candidate was approached to fill the role. But the candidate turned it down because she was based in Reading and had childcare commitments that would not be possible to fulfil because the new role was in London. Despite the fact that her manager had already had a conversation with her about what her ambition and restrictions were, and she had said that she was not able to move due to children's schooling, this had not been taken into account by senior leaders because they hadn't been told by her manager. Her manager thought he could persuade her when the time came. They simply didn't ask the question, or consider that she might turn down promotion. The role remained vacant for some time, as no other candidate was deemed to be suitable, and an external candidate had to be sought at great expense. The vacancy caused operational issues in the department and confidence in the business dropped with shareholders as the perception was that the business was not planning and making contingencies for their people.

If the talent process had been running effectively, then it would have challenged her suitability with her manager much earlier, and the conversation with her about what she really wanted to do would have been noted so that it would have allowed the business to recognise the gap in their plan. Often this doesn't happen because managers think that it is politically incorrect to question someone's commitment, especially women's, because of their responsibility for childcare, other dependants, or commitments. But having an honest conversation with **all** potential successors is vital. In this instance it was a woman, but in just as many cases it will be a man who cannot move for personal reasons. Good talent reviews will honour that honesty and seek to develop the individual in situ, understanding that the personal reasons are genuine and not allowing them to rule out a great candidate for a future move.

4. Problem #4. Failure to identify the risk. Perhaps a more serious failure is that in many businesses the talent and performance process is only used to address leadership and management roles, and yet in some businesses the technical capability in these rapidly changing businesses is even more critical and should be seen as a key component of the process. Where this happens, it can save huge amounts of money and identify risk in a business to both its operating capability and its reputation.

Example:

The newly appointed Managing Director of an 800 person business asked to do a top to bottom review of talent. This was the first time that the business had considered conducting such a review, and because of the nature of the business it decided to review everyone, including key technical staff. During discussions, the conversation turned to a small department where there were three employees who had a key skill which took five years to master.

During the talent review process it came to light that one of the three employees was on long-term sick leave, having had a heart attack; the second was due to retire within the next six months, with no replacement yet identified; and the third was applying for roles elsewhere in the business, because he could see that the team was about to collapse.

The manager had been aware of the problem for some time and had been trying to raise the issue, but had failed to make the case sufficiently clear. He just kept asking for more resource.

As a result of the talent process, the Managing Director authorised the new hire immediately and requested that the employee looking for a new role be asked to take on a more senior role in the team to avoid him leaving.

Without this intervention the business would have failed to deliver on customer agreed Key Performance Indicators (KPIs) and key targets of importance to National Security. The reputation of the business would have been damaged beyond repair and the customer would have been subject to fines amounting to hundreds of thousands of pounds for failing to deliver. In the light of the information being properly laid out during the talent review the directors were able to make an informed decision based on irrefutable evidence.

These types of example demonstrate the way in which talent can fail when improperly used. When it is applied well it should be seen as a risk management tool to defend current market share and expand into new markets. It has a very important role in helping businesses to operate effectively in steady state or achieve their future growth ambition.

In well-run companies the CEO will be asked to present on the talent plan alongside the financials to the Non-Executive Directors on a regular basis, generally once a year. This plan will include how the selection, development and retention of key employees in the business are being handled. In these instances, the share price will respond well because it knows that having a handle on talent, both its opportunities and constraints, is indicative of a well-run business in which senior managers understand how to optimise this crucial strategic lever.

Making the business case

Every business is unique because of the culture and characteristics that have been created by that business, so the advice here is generic and may be different for the organisation in which you work.

All businesses, including charities and not-for-profit organisations, generally have two aims: making money and saving money. Government organisations are rightly obsessed with saving taxpayers' money, or making the most of what resource they have. Many will have to apply for funding and will be called upon to show how the money that has been provided has been spent. Some organisations might be doing both at the same time. Some will be more overt than others, but without some sort of funding, the organisation will cease to exist. The only exception might be a philanthropic venture that is privately funded. So, the starting point for a business case is will it save or make money? If you can answer the questions below and know that this is the most important business issue for the organisation in which you operate, then the rest will flow. It is worthwhile taking a lead from finance departments, as they often write some of the best business cases you will ever see. It would be a highly unusual Finance Director that does not ask for their team to provide the following data for any major spend.

1. How will this initiative fit with the culture (values and behaviour) of the business?

2. What impact will it have on the bottom line?

   a. Will it save money (reduce recruitment costs, lower attrition, retain key players for a longer period of time, etc)?

   b. Will it make money (find a scarce skill that is needed to grow the business, match supply of people with demand, support development that allows growth into new areas of business, create a training programme that requires participants to develop new lines of business)?

3. What is the measure of success for the CEO and the other directors? Find out exactly what their criteria is and use this as the basis for the work that you are proposing.

4. How will you measure and provide evidence of the contribution that the initiative is making (tracking share price, attrition, return to work, promotion, recruitment costs, etc)?

5. How will you communicate this measurement (to whom, when and in what detail)?

6. What are the risks associated with doing this and with not doing this (which competitors you will be competing with, how this will impact brand if you don't do it)?

7. What are the costs (including time taken)?

By building the business case with the leaders in the business on an individual basis, it creates buy in, flushes out ideas that may be helpful to the case and reveals any resistance. Then when it is presented to a group, or the CEO, the case is more likely to gain approval.

Top Tips:

+ Get buy in from the top.

+ Be clear about the business imperative. Does, it make money, or save money?

+ Review talent alongside changing business models.

+ Make sure that talent initiatives are joined up and review them regularly.

+ Measure and provide evidence of progress. What is the Return on Investment?

CHAPTER 3

WHAT IS TALENT?

Demand and supply for the right type of resource in the right quantity and quality already has, or will, become a major issue in most organisations. Even if they have met that challenge for now, most organisations will still face issues of resource constraints at some stage in their evolution. Resource constraints can have serious consequences for a company's ability to meet current and future customer requirements and stay ahead of the competition. As a result, talent acquisition and development have grown in importance in many companies because of the dilemma faced by those businesses.

The first big question faced by many businesses is: 'How do we know what we need?' In the case of current or short-term requirements, the answer to this may appear to be fairly straightforward. That said, Strategic Planning can give you a very different view of those short-term fixes and yet very few companies do it on a regular basis.

Combining the strategic business planning process with resource planning can save millions of pounds, avoid redundancies and allow talent to flourish within a business.

Current business needs are generally identified by managers within an organisation. They find it relatively easy to forecast what is needed, based on their knowledge of the current supply and demand model. But what happens when that model shifts, or the market alters in some way? Managers are often so wrapped up in 'hitting their numbers', cutting costs, or expanding the current business that they do not have time to plan. In some cases, it just may not occur to them that everything is changing or, worse still, they may not see it as their role to adapt to changes. They may also be aware of a potential threat to their operating capability, but not have the platform or the evidence presented in a sufficiently compelling way to make their case.

In the UK several distinct changes in the workplace have taken place that are of strategic importance at both an organisation and socio-economic level:

1. The increase in technology and its impact on current market share.

2. The increasing number of women in the workplace, which has created a need to better balance family and working life for all workers.

3. The changing values of younger workers because of their exposure to technology, which has challenged businesses to think differently.

4. Increasing globalisation of market places brought about by opening up technology and geographical boundaries.

5. Economic instability caused by war, famine and terrorism, which has created uncertainty.

6. The influx of migrant workers, which is now creating tension and territorialism in unforeseen places.

At the time of writing the UK is planning to leave the European Union which has already begun to create tension between different European countries. Old alliances that were based on shaky ground appear to be breaking down. The EU is opposed to the UK breaking away and seems set on ensuring that the UK is held up as an example of what other EU countries must NOT do. On one level this will make it really hard for all of us to just do business with each other, while on another level it may present some new opportunities that had not previously been available. Moving parts, people and products around the region is potentially going to become more costly and time consuming. But more damaging is the impact of the perceptions we hold of each other. Those already working together in cross-border European teams have been shocked and saddened by the decisions made by the UK. Some tension has crept in as people have been asking themselves whether this was what UK colleagues had been thinking all along. A certain mistrust has begun to appear. It is hard enough to create a virtual team where these tensions do not already exist, but now it is becoming increasingly difficult and, if anything, more important.

Teams that have to work across borders will be continuously challenged to consider how they might behave differently, and this will be on top of the very different cultural norms that we know already exist.

Example:

In Milan the MD would dine every day in a room with all of his managers, with the MD serving pasta from a pan to each person in turn. He would then preside over the meal as if he were the father figure. After lunch the whole team had to join him on a walk around the square, then go and have a coffee together before beginning work for the afternoon.

This cultural difference is one small, perhaps insignificant, example of the richness created by different norms. This is now changing. We are seeing a massive shift in how business is done, and the evolution of technology is challenging our view of how business should be conducted. People do business with people, but because of the way that social media is influencing society, there have been subtle, and not so subtle, shifts in how businesses sell to the public or each other. In the advertising sector, spend has declined radically in traditional methods and risen dramatically in social media and technological fixes.

Organisations are using social media to reach their audience. There is a growing trend towards people being more influenced by being able to interact with organisations when they buy, and social trends like BOGOF – Buy One, Get One Free – are growing in numbers. People want to work for organisations who have an online presence and a social conscience.

Marketing in particular has changed beyond recognition. People record their TV programmes and fast forward through ads, paper versions of newspapers are in decline and everything can be bought over the internet. Products that used to only ever be bought on the high street are now more likely to be delivered to your door: food, books, clothes, even cars. You can test drive a virtual car and have it delivered to your door like an Amazon package. People buy based on reviews of others. Buyers might do a little research beforehand to check out product details. They may even visit a store to be able to look, touch and try out items, but then they go home and order online. This is changing the nature of business, and the relationships we have with our own marketing teams, buyers and end users is changing beyond recognition. Digital marketers focus on Black Friday. Graduates are coming out of university wanting to be web designers or game developers. But what is also becoming clear is that you need fewer of these types of people and that their expertise has to be cutting edge. All of this change means that what employees see of organisations that they want to work for, before they have joined, is fundamentally changing.

So, what do people look for in organisations to which they aspire to join? The Chicago School of Sociologists in the early 20th century suggested that individuals are attracted to organisations in which there is a match for their values, career orientation or career anchors. But if it is not visible, then how would an organisation know what is important to those people that they wish to attract? And how do people tap into the culture of the business from outside? Where does responsibility lie for ensuring that the business is evolving its people practices in line with these changes? In many cases it would be argued that this is the role of the HR team (where one exists) to lead this change. But it is also incumbent on all leaders of a business to be aware and mindful of what they need to be doing differently to support and meet the challenge of change. What they do and say is now seen by everyone who has access to the internet and this can make or break a business.

Example:

Companies like Budweiser Beer are pledging to donate money to poor communities to bring them clean water. This social conscience impacts brand awareness and reputation. People want to interact with a business. It is not enough to buy a product and have money donated. So we have seen companies like Innocent drinks who started an internet campaign on Facebook asking people to knit hats for their bottles. These were then sent to Innocent and the bottles sold through a supermarket. But the real destination of those hats was a neo natal unit, where the premature babies needed hats when they were born. Genius marketing because it used social media to spread a viral campaign appealing to the social conscience of customers and getting them involved in corporate, social responsibility agendas.

Interest groups and pressure groups are growing in importance. Particularly in the medical field, they are sometimes more knowledgeable than the so-called experts. That's because they are living with the condition and see it as being in their own interest to do as much research as possible, and to stay up to date with the latest thinking and new developments.

Market sectors are blurring. Hyundai are selling cars on the internet like an Amazon purchase, Ford are setting up digital centres where you can experience driving without actually getting into a car. What business are they in? IT? Travel? Car manufacturing? Entertainment?

It is somewhat of a platitude to state that the pace of change in technology has accelerated to a point where the 'new normal' is a by-word for nothing being stable. The reality is that businesses are having to continually reinvent themselves. The lack of stability and disruption of status quo means that businesses need to focus more on 'what ifs' and to ask the unthinkable question about who, or what, the next 'Category Killer' (Clayton Christensen)[5] might be. Surprisingly few businesses have an R&D focus on their own business models. They may be tracking the competition and looking at what others are doing to threaten market share in the business in which they operate, and yet they do not consider those outside the current competition as being important. In his seminal work on Disruptive Technologies, Christensen identified that new entrants to a market will nearly always win, so we have supermarkets that are also banks and insurance companies that provide plumbing services. What business are they really in? Who are their competitors? Perhaps more importantly, where will they go next? And what talent will they need to build to take them there?

What does all this mean for Talent?

One way in which talent can help to support this innovation and change is by facilitating blue sky thinking techniques that will allow a free flow of ideas to happen. Introducing 'what if' scenario planning, as well as strategic resource planning tools, allows leaders and managers to stand back and ask some questions that may not have occurred to them to ask before. This can be done in a number of different ways.

1. Talent hot housing. Bringing in current experts, customers and diverse minds to challenge by looking at changes in the law, changes in labour markets and demographics, changes in technology, predicted changes in the general economy, anything physically being done with the work environment or upskilling people, is a great starting point to consider the new world.

Example:

A development programme with a primary goal to create change was introduced into a FTSE 100 blue chip organisation. Young apprentices were assigned to management teams as 'Future World Guides'. Their job was to challenge the thinking and input on the technology of the future for the middle managers. The initiative was highly successful, as managers' fed back that the inclusion of someone from a different generation gave them an insight into the potential future needs of employees as well as customer behaviours.

---

2. Thought redirection tools. For example, using a tool such as De Bono's 'six thinking hats'[6] which is a technique that can be used to systematically re-direct thought using Direct Attention Tools. De Bono identified six different ways in which to approach a problem, or an opportunity. Participants in a meeting are invited to deliberately think in a particular way, which allows a more 'productive, focused, and mindfully involved' discussion to evolve. Participants may use any of the six hats: White (facts and only facts), Yellow (value and benefit), Black (difficulties and dangers), Red (emotions and feelings), Green (opportunities and new ideas), and Blue (control mechanism). By using specifically the Green, Yellow

and White ones only, in a particular meeting, and then applying other filters later, businesses can learn to think outside the box and consider what might happen next in their own market, or in other market sectors.

Example:

A talent programme invited participants to take part in imagining the future. They were allowed to think about what they would really like to happen in life to solve real problems. One suggestion was a service that allowed luggage to be transported from your home to your holiday destination without having to carry it. This service now exists in several different formats, not as a direct result of this programme but the idea for such a business was imagined during this process.

---

3. Shadow boards. Giving a group of high potential individuals privileged access to past board papers and asking them to research key competitors as well as one or two other organisations that have a reputation for entering new territory. The group is then invited to form a shadow board or operate as a consultancy which is tasked with producing papers and recommendations on how the business might look.

The output and recommendations from these exercises may not all be feasible, but the thinking will help to jolt current thinking to consider a different reality. This in turn creates questions about what resource might be needed, either to defend current market share or to enter a new market segment. More importantly, where the ideas are adopted and communicated out to the business, it forces current management to forecast very differently around the skill base that they seek to recruit or develop.

This scenario planning might also lead to the identification of significant gaps or overlaps in a business and will certainly help mangers to think differently about what is needed in the future. It is unlikely that it will identify long-term gaps, because the pace of change is so rapid and is not conducive to thinking too far ahead. But where there are clear near to medium-term gaps, the next step is to create a virtual job specification. Again, using the data gathered by the scenario planning exercise and testing this out on experts, it is possible to create a loose sense of some of the skills that might be needed in the future.

A fast and efficient shorthand step to create job specifications is to use O*NET, which is a US-based publicly-available system that allows people to access thousands of job families and capability frameworks. It can be a useful way to quickly cross–check whether something already exists, or will help companies by identifying if the role is totally new. If a role does exist, it can save time and avoid having to re-invent the wheel. A workshop held on June 2015, led by the Institute for Employment Studies, considered whether there would be value in developing a UK version. In a paper that they released[7] they concluded that whilst it would be of significant value, it would be unfeasible to do so from scratch. The US version has been continually developed since 1938 from its original inception as the US Department of Labor's Dictionary of Occupational Titles (DOT). Instead, the workshop agreed that the UK should exploit the US version and adopt a collaborative approach to research and developing it further for the UK market. At the time of writing it is unclear whether this has taken place. The US version is still a good place to start for most businesses trying to determine quickly whether they have a novel role on their hands.

Once a template has been produced it can be piloted with friendly customers to see whether they agree that this is a role that is missing and needed. Agreeing confidentiality upfront ensures that the customer understands that this may not happen, in case you can't find the skills. This will help to avoid negative press and stop competitors stealing an early march on your new ideas. If the pilot group gives the idea a thumbs up, then it can be useful to float this on a website so that followers can provide real time market research. Sometimes one of those followers may be interested enough to pursue the role. By asking them to apply, it will flush out more data on whether skill sets and backgrounds exist that might be suitable for the role.

If no one applies, or you have plenty of applications, but none with the correct skills, then you may need to reconsider your options. Perhaps the role is scarce or experimental, in which case it is better not to ask for CVs, because there isn't any point. Nothing applicants have done to date may be of any relevance whatsoever to this future role. Instead, asking applicants to provide a video application explaining what they think they could bring to the role can be a useful alternative.

It may also be worthwhile using this as a development opportunity. Opening up new roles within a business can be a great morale booster. Not only can it help to redeploy people, but it can also be a useful way to communicate to ensure that everyone knows that the business is facing forwards and they can get involved. Because of this, it is also possible to identify where there are some qualifications and experiences that will be needed in the future for roles that do not yet exist, or that have not got enough students to provide for the demands.

If the skills exist, but you don't have enough of them locally, then by working closely with colleges it is possible to create courses and qualifications quickly. Providing sponsorship for employees to study subjects that are scarce can be a really great way for a business to grow their own people. It can also help to redeploy employees that need to be moved around and will ultimately save money that might otherwise have been spent on severance and recruitment.

> **Example:**
>
> A new skill was identified as being required by a small high tech business. But, because the technology was novel, the business knew that the skills did not exist in the local market to fill the gap. Instead a local college was asked to develop a syllabus that would train up unskilled workers and give them not only the required skills but also a qualification to prove to customers that the individual had been professionally trained. The business had a huge response to the advertisement and very quickly filled the places on the programme. The training consisted of some classroom work and on-the-job evaluation, which meant that not only was the unit operational quite quickly, but the quality was also being assessed and assured on a regular basis by experts.

Clearly the timescales on this are critical, as employees need to have the skills in advance of the business need. So it makes sense for the strategic planning process to be a continuous cycle.

In some very forward thinking businesses that need scarce high level qualifications, they are forecasting so well and so accurately that they are able to reach back to school leavers to encourage them to study the subjects that they have identified will be required in future years before they are needed. This is easier to apply in steady state industries where the type and quantity of resource is predictable and slow to change. It can be more challenging, but not impossible, to make happen in fast-moving enterprises. This ability to influence those outside the traditional workforce to gain skills is already, and will continue to be, critical for those businesses that employ a high number of contingent workers.

Letting people apply for roles on an automated system gives businesses the chance not only to link together vacancies but also development opportunities. In this way, employees and non-employees can apply for funding to attend training programmes as soon as the need has been identified. Reducing the need to forcibly redeploy people into jobs for which they have no training or interest, avoids having to make people redundant and more accurately matches supply and demand.

Top Tips:

+ When recruiting plan for the future as well as current needs.

+ Include in talent reviews key roles, both technical and leadership.

+ Challenge the status quo using key talent.

+ Tap into customers to help you see into the future.

+ Identify who is responsible for future resource planning and make sure that it happens.

CHAPTER 4

WORKING OUT WHAT YOU NEED

It is always surprising when the costly process of recruitment is initiated without clarity about what 'talent' looks like. Yet many hiring managers subscribe to the 'I will know it when I see it' philosophy and begin looking before they have really thought through what they need. In some cases, they will identify the candidate to be offered a job and then look for a hole in the organisation that fits.

Planning what is needed before embarking on the process will help to:

a. Build a scalable business

b. Facilitate business success both now and in the future

c.   Create longevity to appointments and future proof the business

d.   Avoid litigation and costly mistakes

e.   Improve Return On Investment (ROI) on the hiring process

f.   Enable constructive feedback about the outcome with all those who apply

g.   Manage expectations of those within the business

h.   Allow those who aspire to progress to develop the skills needed to do so before they apply

i.   Improve engagement and morale for those who are motivated by career progression

Given that there are so many benefits, the question is, why doesn't it happen? Part of the answer is that it can be difficult to identify what is needed. A role specification that identifies the knowledge, skills and behaviours of the intended role holder is an easy way for managers to think about what it is that they need from the job holder. It doesn't have to be long and complicated. Too often job descriptions are used which have been written as a way for organisations to defend themselves against future litigation by adding in all sorts of extraneous information about health and safety duties, etc. Whilst these may be required for legal purposes they are not meaningful or helpful in practice. Where job descriptions become too corporate and defensive they become discredited, and managers start to create their own versions.

Knowledge is just as it sounds. What are the things that an ideal candidate needs to know in order to do a good job? This might include qualifications or credentials that they have gained by demonstrating their knowledge of how to do something. Passing a written exam, such as the highway-code part of a driving test, might be included in this category.

Skill is more complex to define, as it can sometimes be confused with behaviours. To simplify things, it is better to be considered as the skills that a job holder must be able to exhibit in order to do a job, e.g. being able to sail a boat or interpret a set of accounts.

Behaviours include the way in which someone operates. It is often confused with skill but it happens at a deeper level. It can often reflect someone's value set. Being open to criticism, truthful and confident are all types of behaviours.

Once knowledge, skills and behaviours have been identified for a role the next step is to define what 'good' looks like. It is important to set a bar, so that candidates are able to be measured against an independent measure and not against each other. This may be open to debate, as ultimately you will be deciding which candidate best fits the brief. It is important that it is an absolute measure rather than a direct comparison which might give rise to allegations of discrimination, even where there are none, and litigation is likely to follow. Managers are often surprised to know that the only time someone outside an organisation can take them to a tribunal is for discrimination during recruitment.

A well regarded method is called a Repertory Grid Interview. It is used to identify what good looks like from a number of perspectives and then create a framework. To do this, you conduct a series of interviews to determine what good looks like and what poor looks like, then use this information to construct a framework that allows hiring managers and anyone else who is interested to identify what the organisation means by 'good' or 'poor'. It is helpful for this to be shown as the different stages in the development of a role, so that managers can identify and describe what the gradations in between look like as well. Whilst this sounds straightforward, it isn't. It can be very hard for an internal person to suspend judgment. Using an impartial observer is the most effective way to get this done.

Once developed, a clear definition is a valuable tool, because it can be used for hiring decisions, promotion, performance management as well as talent discussions. The downside is that clear definitions need to be written in a way that allows them to withstand changes, possibly on a regular basis. But the advantage of them is that managers are invariably more confident about having difficult conversations because they have a tangible more objective framework to use in order to explain their feedback. Employees love the clarity because it helps them to see what they need to do both now and if they want to be promoted in the future, and this can have a significant positive impact on morale.

Example:

A finance company was using a performance management system that was hugely discredited. The employee would be invited in by the manager and told 'You are a 4', with no explanation about what that meant. Satisfaction amongst fee earning employees was at an all-time low with only 23% of the employees being happy with the appraisal system.

As a result of this unhappiness, the business introduced a bespoke performance management system incorporating a separation of 'what' and 'how'. 'What' was defined as the actual work itself. 'How' was defined by behavioural indicators. For each level of role within the business, a bi-polar framework was produced that defined 'good' and 'bad' performance. After implementation of this, alongside other measures, the satisfaction rating for the appraisal system increased to 71%.

In many ways technical roles are easier to define (unless they are entirely new), because it can be simpler to determine the progression in knowledge, skills and behaviours that are required as a job holder becomes increasingly expert. Leadership competencies, on the other hand, pose an altogether more challenging problem, as we shall see in a later chapter. To start with there is a great deal of debate about whether they should be called competencies or capabilities. This has resulted in the terms competency and capability being used interchangeably and in fact there is no evidence to show that they are different concepts.

The idea of competencies began in the 1970s with the work of David McClelland at the McBer consultancy. The primary reason that organisations persist in developing their own version is that their unique blend of values and the strategic direction of different businesses varies enormously. This suggests that the combination of what is important, or a high priority, may vary between different businesses, even within the same sector. This might be the reason that research found evidence that leadership 'talent' in one organisation does not always transfer successfully into other organisations. This implies that the identification of talented leaders can only be done on a bespoke basis within a company.

The implication for organisations here is that they should not rely on the talent rating that a new hire has been given by their old company, because it is unlikely that they will be judged in the same way by the new company. This might be a contentious view, but it might also explain why churn in senior appointments happens when someone is appointed through the 'old boy network' rather than going through the normal channels, and they then turn out to be a bit of a disappointment. The recommendation would be to judge the new hire on their own merits through a properly objective process, rather than rely on hearsay. Many consulting organisations offer a hiring profile service for a senior appointment.

One note of caution here is that global organisations need to be careful in constructing frameworks that are heavily biased towards a particular geography and applying this universally. What is regarded as 'talent' in one country may not be regarded in the same way in a different culture.

Example:

A global firm hired an organisation to do some work on its global businesses where a 360 tool was used across different geographies. This tool had been designed in the UK through robust processes. To use it in Russia it was simply translated into Russian. When the results were being reviewed it became clear that 'self-confidence' appeared to be low in Russia. The management team in the UK created all sorts of explanations for this and ended up concluding that the Russian management team needed to work on this area in order to improve their performance. This was despite the fact that Russia was already a high performing region. When the results were shared with the Russian management team a very different view became apparent. The Russians were very pleased that the self-confidence results were low. Their view was that 'standing out from the crowd' is not a positive concept. Anyone who appeared 'self-confident' would not do well in Russian business because they would be seen to be not working as part of a team.

If the organisation had created a bespoke questionnaire for what was needed in Russia, rather than simply taking a UK version and translating it into a different language, they would have received a very different result. Ignoring cultural nuances and overtones might have led to them overlooking the real stars in Russia and forcing the managers into hiring and developing a team who would conform to the UK norms and probably fail in delivering high performance in Russia.

The case for diversity

Diversity encompasses many varieties of 'difference' in a population. At one level this definition reflects the difficulty of defining diversity, and it does not capture the continuum of differences even on one parameter; we are beginning to see this in regard to discussion about transgender populations, what does female or male even mean? Not all people who are categorised as one gender are the same. It also fails to convey the true complexity created by overlapping categories or, as researchers[8] describe them, 'fault lines', where one type of diversity crosses over with another; for example, how do you define black females? This area of work has been very under researched and organisations are only now beginning to get to grips with what it might mean for them. It is generally acknowledged that diversity in a workforce is a good thing, but what is the evidence for this belief?

Studies[9] have shown that diversity does improve financial targets like productivity, return on equity and market performance. Increasingly a growing number of businesses are focused on not fitting candidates to company culture, but encouraging diversity and difference to deliver creative tension and drive business advantage. However, evidence does not make it clear whether the link between business performance and diversity may be as a result of other factors, such as the size of the business. Perhaps larger businesses do better because they can devote more resources and more time to getting it right.

Much of the evidence to date has been focused on gender diversity, where research shows that, whilst it has a positive impact on business, diversity imbalance is changing very slowly in most organisations. One reason for this might lie in some recent research conducted in the USA which has shown that there is inherent discrimination based on stereotypes of appropriate employees to promote. The Pew Institute found that as recently as 2015[10] the majority of Americans believe that women are every bit as capable of being good political leaders as men and able to dominate the corporate boardroom, but that women do not become leaders due to a difference in perceived capability. Their research showed that it is this perception that appears to be driving inequality because it continues to be maintained, despite the fact that women were indistinguishable from men on key leadership traits such as intelligence and capacity for innovation. Furthermore, respondents believed that women are more compassionate and better organised than men which were considered to be key leadership skills, and yet were still not being elected.

Their research suggests that in the USA at least, double standards are being applied to women seeking to climb to the highest levels of either politics or business and that there is a belief that women have to do more than their male counterparts to prove themselves.

Perhaps of more concern is the suggestion, from their research, that the public is divided about whether, despite the major advances women have made in the workplace, the imbalance in corporate America will change in the foreseeable future. About half (53%) believe men will continue to hold more top executive positions in business in the future; 44% say it is only a matter of time before as many women are in top executive positions as men. Americans are less doubtful when it comes to politics: 73% expect to see a female president in their lifetime, and yet in the 2016 US Presidential election Hillary Clinton failed to be elected despite holding a majority in the popular vote.

In the UK and Australia more progress is being made. The Women on Boards (WOB) initiative has had some success in addressing gender equality through supporting women by coaching them on how to apply for roles on boards in the UK and Australia (FTSE 100 women on boards rose from 12.5% in 2011 to 23% in 2015 and FTSE 250 from 7.8% in 2011 to 17.7% in 2015), and have been working hard on the Davies Report outputs to address these perceived inequalities.

There is less research in other areas of diversity, perhaps as a result of the fact that there are fewer examples in corporate life to study. Research[11] shows that creative tension and difference of opinions may lead to an organisation where innovation and group work outputs are improved. The conclusion is that difference is positive in the workplace and that is what organisations such as Pandora are seeking to address.

Example:

Organisations such as Pandora are now referring to 'culture add'. Their view is that increasing the mix of diversity will form the basis of competitive advantage for businesses, and that making use of the full complement of talent is the best way to capitalise on this resource. They deliberately avoid recruiting people who 'fit' their culture and instead seek out those who do not fit the mould.

What does this mean for the Talent agenda? It means that any talent work must be completed in the context of what is happening in the world, and that whilst positive discrimination is illegal, positive action can be used in recruitment. Balanced lists of candidates can be requested from head hunters which show a representative sample of the population. This has been the practice in many businesses and yet diversity is still not at the levels to which most businesses aspire. To understand this it might be helpful to consider what might be undermining progress.

Unconscious bias

Unconscious bias is a term used to describe bias that we are unaware of: it happens outside of our control. It is a biological response to stimuli and happens automatically. It occurs when our brain makes quick judgments and assessments of people and situations. We all form opinions and hold beliefs based on something called 'social categorisation'. This is an instinctive biological process in which we rapidly sort people into groups rather than think of each as unique.

There are many reasons that categorisation happens. It saves us time and effort because it is quick and easy to do, so it saves the brain from constantly sorting individual pieces of data on a continuous basis. It makes us feel more comfortable because it helps us to understand what responses may be expected from us and how others are likely to behave or respond as a result. We tend to use categories such as our culture, environment, gender, experiences to date.

We build prejudices through how we experience the world. We may not be fully aware of what is happening because we absorb information from many sources, generally family, friends and the media. This happens on a continuous basis. Through prejudice we may make invalid assumptions about others, both positive and negative, because we categorise other people as a 'type' and fail to see them as a unique individual.

Whilst categorisation is a helpful biological mechanism for us as individuals, prejudices are not. Holding them strongly will sometimes have unforeseen and often undesirable consequences for both individuals as well as organisations.

> **Example:**
>
> In one consultancy business in London the post room had huge turnover. Attrition was running at 66%, and the vast majority were new team members who on average lasted for six months before leaving. Generally, if they made it past this point then they would stay long term. The Senior Leaders had decided that the 'problem' needed to be investigated. They believed that new employees were finding it difficult to settle in because the main post room was below ground and had no natural light. However, through interviews it came to light that the main issue was that the team, who had all been working together for many years, all supported one London football team. Any new joiner was interrogated by the team, and if they supported a different football team was made to feel so isolated that they resigned. This closed-shop thinking, which was built on a belief that only those supporters of that particular football club should be employed, was driving suitable candidates out of the business for all the wrong reasons and causing operational issues for the firm. The categorisation had created an inappropriate prejudice that was harming both individuals and the organisation alike.

As illustrated in this example, values and beliefs are likely to be deeply held, strongly defended and difficult to change. When presented with an example that challenges a person's values, the individual is likely to label this as 'atypical' rather than change their beliefs. The reason for this is that we use our values to construct our own identity and so an attack on our values will be seen as an attack on us. Telling people to 'not be biased' or that 'diversity is good' will not change behaviour, because it does not change beliefs.

As a society we are biased towards protecting and defending those who are like us and rejecting those who are not. Thus cliques and barriers are formed that the 'out' group find it hard to penetrate, as in the post room/ football team example. This may lead to organisations in which the 'corporate type' predominates, creating a blinkered view of how to do business and who should be selected or promoted.

Accepting that we all have biases and determining how these help or hinder an individual, team or organisation is the first step in making change happen. There are questionnaires that can be used to surface what those views might be, but making the case for change can prove challenging, in particular where an individual or organisation has been successful through holding those views. Using research data and facts will help to realign inappropriately held strong views and biases, but may not entirely change them.

In the new more fluid business model prejudice might be seen where there is a mixture of permanent and temporary workers. Research[12] has shown that where this occurs, in particular where permanent employees have left and returned on a different contract but doing the same work, there was a worsening of relations between managers and employees. Both types of workers perceived that there was a difference in the way managers treated them and both parties felt unfairly treated. As a result there was a decrease in permanent employees' loyalty, and an increase in their interest both to leave and /or join a union. So re-employing permanent staff who have left the business and wish to re-join on a temporary contract can have a detrimental effect on morale for all concerned. The question is, how does a talent process that attempts to open its parameters to temporary or contract staff do so without having a detrimental impact on the permanent employee population?

Top Tips:

+ Identify what 'great' looks like using a framework such as 'knowledge, skills and behaviours'.

+ Review and identify culture bias in talent processes.

+ Consider using diversity to drive innovation and performance.

+ Review unconscious bias and where possible make it conscious and manage it appropriately to eliminate or mitigate it.

+ Prepare for the impact on permanent employees if you are planning to extend talent pool membership to those who are not permanent.

CHAPTER 5

FINDING TALENT

Attracting talent

In very technical organisations, where new skills and capabilities are needed on a continuous basis, it might be challenging to get external candidates to apply in the first place.

Ensuring that those who apply are of the right calibre and able to do the job becomes increasingly difficult when managers themselves do not really know anything about the newest technology that is being sought. In these instances a more pragmatic approach might be adopted.

1. Using a panel of interviewees who are experts in the field can be a useful way to avoid situations where interviewees are being lost because it takes too long for decisions to be made. Sometimes the business of selecting the right candidate becomes a secondary consideration with the process becoming elongated as more and more people want to interrogate the person and lose sight of the main purpose of the interview. For all the best reasons, 'technical experts' can get so carried away that they put in too many interviewers because of their interest in the subject. They can get carried away with asking in-depth questions, or reveal more about what they are working on than they should.

Example:

A scientific company appeared to be having great difficulty recruiting a candidate to join their team. The candidates were invited to come in and present their research findings to the senior players on four or five occasions to increasingly larger audiences, and interviews were being conducted by more and more people. The whole process was taking up to three to four months, and when an offer was finally made the candidates were turning it down, or had pulled out prematurely because they had already been offered a role by a rival firm. The whole process was taking far too long, the operation was suffering and the reputation of the business was at stake.

It transpired that the recruitment process had morphed into a fact-finding mission, with other researchers being inappropriately invited to attend in order to update themselves on the latest research, rather than taking part in a selection process. As a result the business was losing money because the process was slowing down operations and wasting a huge amount in management time. A panel of appropriately trained managers was appointed. Time taken to offer, cost of time taken to offer, and conversion rates from interview to offer all improved significantly.

The reputation of the company improved as word got round that candidates weren't going to be grilled or exploited for their knowledge during quasi seminars and more candidates began to apply.

2. Use business psychologists to short list according to the values and behaviours of the candidate. This can be a useful way to have someone independent challenge the 'fit'. An independent expert can ask questions about how the culture may be impacted, or experienced by new recruits. They can also challenge when a culture is becoming too strong and more diversity might be advisable. Generally a report would be generated that provides a view of the 'fit' with the organisation, as well as the ability to do the role. The report allows an organisation to make a choice knowing how closely the candidate fits the culture of the business. This culture fit can be critical, especially with very technical roles, as the candidate will still need to fully function as a part of the organisation. In some businesses this is the main criteria for selection and might be part of an overall strategy to strengthen or change a culture. Some organisations believe that the technical skills can be taught but interpersonal skills, values and behaviours are either a fit or not.

A report is also a really useful tool to feedback to candidates, successful and otherwise, to be used for development purposes at a later date.

Example:

In one merchant bank they select employees on the basis of values and behaviours, not skills, and then hire candidates predominantly on a fixed-term contract for six months before making them permanent or terminating. This allows the organisation and the candidate a cooling-off period, so that the two parties can eyeball each other in real life scenarios. But once permanent, the employee is there for the long haul.

The view taken by the bank is that the employee is placed in a role that best fits their skills. If this is not successful, they will move the person to a different role, believing that the employee is a good fit for the business but has not yet found their niche. As an example, they moved one individual back to Hong Kong because she needed to be there for family reasons. It was also true that the role she was holding in London was not a great fit and she had been struggling to achieve high performance. The bank was able to accommodate her personal needs, but more importantly the business would not let her fail in the role she was in because then the whole business would suffer.

The philosophy was simple: 'If one fails, we all fail'. Interestingly, employee engagement, profitability and share price at the bank were all very high and remain so.

3. In organisations where soft skills are important, but what the business is looking for is cutting-edge thinking in a new area, then attracting and selecting the right candidate becomes incredibly challenging. If you have never seen the new technology working, how will you know whether the candidate in front of you is capable and the best in the field? One solution here is to use temporary placements.

> **Example:**
>
> Blue sky thinking was not readily available in this organisation. But the business needed continuous access to cutting-edge ideas, but once the candidate has joined and then completed their research they may subsequently lose their desire to innovate and the business would be committed to the researcher with no fresh ideas. So, to get around this, a three-year post-doc internship was introduced. This gave candidates funding and support for their studies and the business a steady stream of new research targets. After three years the individual could apply to join the business, extend the contract or leave, depending upon the needs of the business and the individual concerned. Similar models have been introduced through internship routes.

4. The growth of social media has made referrals easier, and at the same time more difficult, to attract and identify talent. Candidates have access to all sorts of information about an organisation. Social media sites such as Glassdoor can either help or hinder a growing business. One utility business very successfully used Glassdoor to help them retrieve their reputation and thus their ability to attract high calibre candidates. But it can just as easily go the other way.

Remembering that the hiring process is a two-way process has become increasingly critical where scarce resource and limited talent pools are concerned. Finding out where the people are that you want to attract has become complex. In particular this is true of 'millennials', that mysterious category of candidates who are younger and supposedly much more tech savvy than older candidates. One way to determine how to access these candidates is to ask. In one telecommunications business they have invited their employees' sons, daughters and friends to come to a focus group to discover where and for what they are seeking a role.

So how are things changing? Research reports by PwC in 2011 and 2014[13] have both alluded to a difference in the way that young people see work. Through their survey they stated that expectations of how long millennials thought they wanted to stay in a job were based on what they had seen happen to their parents. There was a sense that they would not offer loyalty because they did not expect to get it back. This need to be self-reliant meant that they were more flexible about what they would do, but in return they wanted to be developed, so that they had something to offer a future employer. The survey also showed that time was more important than money because they wanted the opportunity to have a life outside of work. Some of them were developing their own businesses to give them some sort of security for the future. Work-life balance was also high on the agenda because they wanted to work hard and play hard. They found that they were ambitious and expected to move up the ladder very fast. They reported that they were keen to travel, but to safe Western-style countries and not countries such as Brazil, Russia, India and China (BRIC countries). Surprisingly, a Social Responsibility agenda which had previously been high on the millennials' wish list was not as important as working for a brand that was recognised and highly regarded. One major difference that was found was that millennials were much more aware of diversity and were very judgmental of what was said and done in this area. They were very alert to words not matching deeds, seeing it as hypocritical.

This study has been challenged by other researchers, most notably a recent Harvard Business Review article[14] which cited research[15] showing that there is very little discernible difference between generations and that those that do exist are probably a feature of the stage of life, rather than a generational difference. In the same HBR article they also cited IBM's 2015 report[16] which shows that the following are important to all generations in the same descending order:

1. Making a positive impact on my organisation

2. Help solve social and/or environmental challenges

3. Work with a diverse group of people

4. Work for an organisation among the best in my industry

5. Do work I am passionate about

6. Become an expert in my field

7. Manage my work-life balance

8. Become a senior leader

9. Achieve financial security

10. Start my own business

Attracting talent may need to be more technically sophisticated to keep up with the changes which we are all experiencing. This applies universally and not because of the needs of one particular generation. Messages about the different ways in which millennials behave, how they want to be treated and, more importantly, what they are looking for from a career may not be that dissimilar from what we all want. This might be good news for businesses who are getting it right, as they can continue to do what they have always done. For those businesses who are struggling to find the right candidate for their business, then this list might provide a useful template against which to compare how well they are getting the right messages across to their audience.

What is not clear is whether this is true for those who follow non-standard career paths. This seems to be an area where more research would be useful if organisations are to capitalise on this resource pool.

Identifying talent

For those who are getting it right and attracting a huge number of candidates and in sectors that are not short of candidates, organisations have to put in a lot of effort to sift out and select the right people from all those who have applied. To do this, many organisations use automated filters to make the job of finding the right people easier to achieve. Organisations like GCHQ are appealing to candidates through gaming and problem solving to attract the kind of candidate that they want to apply. They are using the relationship that people have with technology as an attraction and candidate capture mechanism.

The easiest and perhaps bluntest instrument to use is a psychometric test. This can give an early indication of suitability but needs to be used with caution. Many organisations have moved away from ability tests that measures cognitive functioning such as numerical and verbal reasoning because research has shown repeatedly[17] that in some cases these are unfairly biased against certain groups in society. Instead, they use automated 'killer questions' and situational judgment tests produced by qualified test providers and psychologists to identify suitable candidates and then invite them to attend an assessment centre where they can demonstrate the application of their knowledge. This allows high quality mass screening to take place without discrimination.

By running assessment centres more people can be involved in the decision, and the right training for assessors can help to enhance the decision. It can also help in further talent identification, as different managers are involved and able to see the standard of new hires being brought into other departments which may be different from their own. Getting the whole team involved in the selection decision can support decisions that lead to the business selecting people with the right fit for the team. One drinks company has employed this method of recruitment very successfully for many years. The success has been outstanding. However, the introduction of a team selection process needs to be handled carefully to ensure that it does not have an unforeseen negative impact.

Example:

Turnover in the first 90 days for senior hires was very high, as they struggled to fit in, doubted their decision to join and were still in contact with other head hunters who were continuing to explore alternative options for them. To address this, in one consulting firm senior hires are provided with a detailed written report produced during the selection process and an executive coach for the first 90 days to help them to address gaps and to develop a strategy for continuing to develop themselves. This has helped the new hires to make the transition more smoothly and has reduced early-day turnover.

Sadly, very few organisations provide feedback to candidates after they have been appointed. In some consulting firms individuals are provided with an automated report of their feedback post interview. This can be done very simply and cheaply. Where the recruitment and development systems are both automated and talk to each other, the new hire can then access not only the feedback, but different ways in which this maps onto development tools and opportunities that they can access, such as coaching and on-line training or training courses.

Top Tips:

+ Use panels of trained experts.

+ Request professional reports for key hires.

+ Understand and monitor your reputation as an employer.

+ Don't treat millennials any differently from other employees.

+ Actively manage the first 90 days to avoid fallout.

CHAPTER 6

PROMOTING TALENT

If identifying high-potential external candidates is difficult, then it seems that it is even more difficult to do so with internal candidates, because bias and reputation begin to influence decision making. Many organisations will have a talent and succession process that allows managers to put forward their own succession plan and identify talent in their teams for the wider organisation to consider for further progression. It is partly that 'further progression' that seems to cause some of the problems.

The talent and succession process varies between different types of organisations, but many companies now favour the 9 box matrix. This is a format that allows the business to plot individuals onto a chart that shows them where someone might fit according to their performance as well as their potential. Many models exist, but the one shown on the next page is fairly typical:

9 Box Matrix

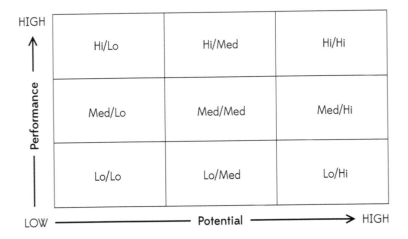

Some organisations are experimenting with a 4 box matrix, as they believe that a 9 box matrix is over complicated and takes too long for managers to understand and complete.

4 Box Matrix

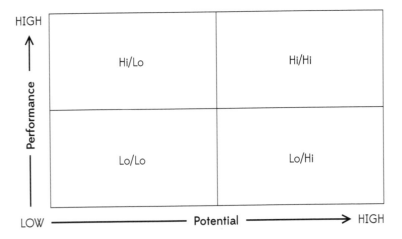

The 4 box matrix has been criticised for being overly simplistic and not providing enough detail to differentiate between individuals. Users begin to start adding in layers of definition and explanation to help justify the decisions they are making.

The resistance to the concept of a 9 box or even a 4 box matrix appears to lie in the word 'box'. Organisations are increasingly reluctant to label people and put them in categories, preferring to see individuals positioned along a continuum. A simple way to overcome this reluctance to labelling may be by plotting individuals on a scattergram, which shows where individuals sit in relation to performance and potential.

Scattergram

This allows there to be greater interpretation of the nuanced differences that may be drawn by where someone sits on the continuum. The disadvantage of plotting individuals in such a way is that there is a temptation to draw a comparison between the other individuals plotted around that space, rather than against the criteria that have been agreed for what the points on the axes mean. The likelihood is that you may end up measuring individuals against one another, rather than against the criteria relating to each axis. This may mean that decisions are based on the wrong criteria.

Whichever model you use, it will always rely on an understanding and interpretation of what each axis is really interested in measuring, and it needs to deliver several things.

Need #1. It needs to map onto the performance review rating of an individual. This is becoming increasingly challenging as businesses are opting to move away from any formal performance review process. One way of doing this is to consider economic worth to the organisation as a way to differentiate between individuals. This helps the business to think about the value of employees in a very direct way. There are many different ways to perform this calculation, but simply taking the total remuneration package and performance rating, then plotting this on the chart with a Red, Amber, Green (RAG) status, will quickly identify where there is a mismatch between those who are underperforming and highlight whether the business is getting value for money. The main reason to stick with a 9 box matrix is that it makes it much easier to differentiate between High, Medium and Low for both performance and potential. However, it can be helpful to mirror the exact performance ratings used in a business so that you do not have to go through a complicated translation of what it all means and how it all fits when plotting it into a different model.

Example:

In one organisation they had five performance review ratings. This made it very difficult for managers to 'guess' the performance rating that they needed to allocate to their employee where a 9 box matrix was being used. They got around this by using a 15 box matrix, thus reducing the work for managers, who only had to focus on getting the potential rating right. It improved credibility and allowed more meaningful discussion to take place.

Need #2. The business needs to be able to identify what is meant by potential:

a. Number of positions. In some companies this is interpreted as being able to step up, zero to one (low potential), two (medium potential) or three (high potential) positions beyond where they currently fit. Clearly the challenge with this is that as you reach the top of the organisation your potential becomes more limited, which is probably not entirely fair but in this context may be accurate.

b. Length of time. In other organisations it is an indication of how many years the person will take to progress further. This turns the matrix on its head, and so those in the one category (i.e. will take one year) may be higher potential than those who will take two years, etc. However, this then creates complications when you have individuals who are close to progression but will not go any further versus those who may be several years off but will go higher.

c. Criteria based. In the best version I have seen it is used as an indicator of a looser, more subjective view of whether the manager believes that the person is capable of more. The clearer the definition, the easier it will be to compare across the business. But this subjective approach has many advantages, as it counters some of the problems I have just described and, provided there is a robust calibration and challenge process, allows for the true long-term picture to emerge.

As I have just demonstrated, 'potential' is highly subjective and not a universally agreed concept. This means that if an employee is considered to be 'talent' in one organisation, they may not appear to be so when they move to a different organisation. This can make life very confusing, not only for the hiring manager but also for the new hire. They may both have unrealistic expectations of successful transfers that fail to materialise. The one exception to this seems to be where the new business has similar values and behaviour to the old.

So how does the business determine who is and is not 'talent'? Generally, the view is that managers are best placed to make that judgment, so the process of identification, communication (if appropriate) and implementation revolves around them. This thinking is necessary and at the same time flawed. The view of a manager will be very influenced by several factors. They may be an extremely good judge of talent in their own teams, or they may not. What will be critical is the backing of senior managers, the espoused and believed purpose of the talent review in that organisation, and what managers believe. Much of this hinges on what the manager sees happen as a result of their talent review. This difference in belief may lead to any one of the following persona being adopted by the manager.

a. The Keeper: 'I know who is talented in my team, but I am not going to tell you because I do not want to lose my top performer.'

This manager will 'sit on' their talent because they believe, rightly or wrongly, that the identification of their team member as 'talent' will mean that the employee is whisked away to join another team. So it's best not to say. You usually see this in businesses where resource is limited and recruitment freezes mean that losing a brilliant team member will not lead to a replacement being provided.

b. The Jealous one: 'I know, but I am not going to tell you because I am jealous of my talented team member. I am insecure about my own capability and think that they are better than me.'

This manager may have been in a business in which they have not been identified as 'talent' and feel resentful of the opportunities that are being provided. They will not offer up talent because they do not want others to overtake them in progressing to the top and are afraid that their team members are better than they are.

c.   The Egoist: 'I am going to tell you that my whole team is brilliant. Because I have been told that my bonus depends upon it and believe that it reflects well on me.'

This manager does not have a true grasp of what good looks like, or may have a team where performance is indeed great, but this does not necessarily mean that all the employees have high potential. Sometimes explaining the difference is all that is required to help the manager to see the difference. At times a direct challenge can be necessary by a more senior executive asking for specific examples to illustrate their view.

d.   The Spartan: 'I do not think that anyone in my team is great because I am very hard on them.'

This manager genuinely believes that the quality of his team is not very good. They may have very high standards for themselves and for everyone around them. This can make it tricky to get them to see their team in a positive light. Putting the team through an assessment centre and comparing them with others can be helpful to provide a benchmark that everyone can use to assess.

e.   The Short-sighted: 'I do not consider future needs of the business, only current needs of the business, when I recruit.'

This manager may be recruiting high calibre recruits, but they only stay for a short period of time because they have been brought in to do a job of work and do not necessarily have the potential to progress. Or worse still, they stay, in the belief that they will have a future career in the business, but it is clear that they are not going to make the grade. This can become an issue where the individuals become disillusioned but do not have the capability or intention to move on either internally or to another company. Effectively, they may be blocking progression for those below them, and this can create some serious consequences in a team because succession is limited. The knock-on impact of potentially losing individuals with knowledge and experience at a later date, when inevitably an external successor has to be brought in, can destabilise the team and in some cases the business. Helping managers by providing training and clear guidelines to explain their role in recruiting for both current and future performance can avert later issues surfacing.

f. The Tactician: 'I genuinely do not have talent in my teams because I just need them to do their job and do not want them to think about the future. That's not my job.'

This manager is more problematic, because although they understand the need to look for potential and performance, they do not want to do so. This generally happens where the technical skills being sought are scarce, or the manager genuinely (possibly rightly) believes that the pool in which they are searching does not have candidates with both. This might be because they cannot wait for the right candidate to appear and so 'bums on seats' becomes the order of the day. Involving this type of manager in a talent and succession planning session early on with their own manager can help to unblock this thinking. It can also be helpful to provide solid data on the demographics that will help to identify where potential candidates might truly be rare and the manager in this case has a point.

Open or closed?

In some organisations, everyone will know that there is a talent pool and who is in it. Other organisations choose to allow employees to voluntarily apply to join the talent pool. In yet others, they can only be nominated for the talent pool by their managers. In some organisations the management team and the individual will know that the employee is in the talent pool, but others will not. In yet other organisations, the management team will know who is in the talent pool but no one else, not even the individual, will know that they are considered to be 'talent'.

The reason that organisations sometimes choose to make it 'closed', i.e. not public knowledge, is that some people see it as elitist and believe that this can make it divisive. Others see it as aspirational and the best way to grow a business. There are distinct advantages and disadvantages to both. And it will depend upon the values held by the business as to which one is chosen.

One reason that there may be good cause for concern about the decision to make it open is illustrated by the controversial work of Jane Elliott in the 1960s[18]. In her experiment, she demonstrated how, by simply labelling participants as inferior or superior based solely upon the colour of their eyes, it exposed them to the experience of being superior or inferior. Whilst this research was aimed at exposing the impact of racial prejudice in schools, what it also exposed is that the group who were consistently told that they were not performing eventually lived up to the expectations held of them. For some people, membership of any group that bestows favour on an 'in-group' is divisive. For that reason, some organisations may choose to keep talent membership a closed exercise. But what is equally, if not more, damaging is the impact on those who believe that they are not valued by the business because they are not considered to be 'talent'. This might be the vast majority of your business and, if badly handled, they will begin to believe and act in a way that they think they are seen, i.e. not 'talented', and if not well handled, this can become the reality in an organisation. For this reason, some businesses choose not to adopt talent identification practices at all, or if they do so, it will happen behind closed doors and may never be overtly discussed with the individual.

If the business has decided that it will use talent identification processes to grow or shape itself and make it known about or not, then it will need to consider what investment this will represent. Regardless of whether membership of a pool is known about, it is critical that something then happens as a result of this being the case. Otherwise, one could argue that the entire process is a waste of time. But without it, the business risks not being ready to change shape or grow.

Where membership is open but nothing happens as a result of being in the pool, it becomes meaningless for the individual and discredited across the business. Where membership of the talent pool is closed, it is not a question of the individual having a poor view of membership, but if the decision is taken to 'do something' with the members, it is critical that this should be explained properly or it can have a complicated and sometimes detrimental impact.

Example:

In a finance company one of the identified high potentials nearly resigned because he was invited to attend a leadership development programme that was designed to accelerate his progress. But no one had told him why he was being invited to attend and he read into it that he was doing something wrong, so thought the programme was remedial. He had not been told there was an issue with his performance, in fact his manager had said nothing to him at all, so he just assumed.

In organisations where membership of the talent pool is known about it needs to be well handled. One way in which to mitigate divisive behaviour is to make part of the requirement that members be reappointed to the pool on an annual basis. Relationships and behaviours can be positively shaped so that members of the talent pool know that they must show humility and actively give something back to the organisation in terms of developing others. If they do not do so, then they will be told that they have been dropped from the talent pool. And nobody wants that to happen.

Just as in Elliott's work, where people began to believe what they were told, the same is true in organisations. It is evident that where the truly talented are identified in small numbers, and there are high levels of agreement that they are the leaders of the future, or that they are critical to the future success of the business, then there is likely to be less self-doubt and issues of equity raised in people's minds. Equally, where it is a pool that is filled on a voluntary basis and there is no threshold to entry, then the general population is less likely to question it. However, in organisations where the pool is wide, the criteria for entry are not well understood or have been applied inconsistently, then the reaction to membership will be less favourable, with employees questioning the validity of membership and seeking to undermine the value of the pool to the organisation as well as to the individual.

There are several ways to counter this type of corporate jealousy. One of which is to raise the bar high and introduce an entry process. This will help where there is a need to ensure that the business is comparing apples with apples, for example in a leadership talent pool. There are risks associated with both having an assessment and not. In these types of interventions communication is critical. If the delegate has been told by their manager that they are considered to be 'talent' and then the assessment suggests otherwise, this can trigger some of the 'out group' mentality that has been referred to previously. However, by creating a benchmark and applying it in a fair and consistent manner, the talent pool may feel that they have earned the right to be there and others will feel better disposed to its existence. Sometimes those not invited will be grateful that they have not been subjected to high levels of scrutiny.

Sometimes organisations make the mistake of thinking that the talent agenda should only be focused on the few elite souls who populate the top right hand corner boxes of the 9 box grid, those who are considered to be high performers and high potential. Admittedly, this is where most organisations choose to focus, because they believe that the greatest return on investment will come from this strategy. Generally, this is a favoured approach in organisations where resource is limited and the talent budget has to be targeted. However, an alternative approach would be to map the whole organisation onto the matrix and talk about this freely with individuals, so that they can see where they fit and what they would need to do to move into a box that would trigger them being considered in a 'talent' pool. Organisations can also choose to offer different 'rewards' in each of the boxes.

Example:

A retail bank chose to focus attention on the central box, where the majority of employees were positioned. Their view was that this represented the majority of the business and that these were people who were powering the engine room at the heart of their business. The purpose of this talent initiative was clearly to engage and inspire the group of medium performers with medium potential to raise their game. As a strategy to improve performance across the organisation it was successful because that was the need of the business at that particular point in time.

A different tactic is for organisations to make talent pool membership quite onerous, so that on the one hand it is considered to be an honour, but on the other hand it comes with lots of conditions and trade-offs, so that the talented employee does not become over confident and develop an 'expectation' mentality. Where this is the case there is usually no requirement for people to agree to be part of the group. They can opt out, but it is worthwhile bearing in mind that where individuals have been identified they can feel under enormous pressure to accept and agree to whatever is needed. One area in particular that can be difficult to negotiate is where the requirement is for talent pool members to agree to move around geographically. In particular, those who have responsibility for childcare or elderly dependants can come under pressure to agree to be in the talent pool, but when they are asked to move to a new assignment are not able to fulfil that request. For that reason, some organisations choose to build in an opt-out clause for a certain period of time. In other cases, talent pool members can opt into a sub category where extra flexibility is required by the business, for which a bonus is allocated. This flexibility allows those who have been identified as talent to be more in control of their careers and navigate personal circumstances.

External talent pools

Market mapping is a process in which hypothetical data is collected about individuals who work for similar organisations, in similar roles, often with competitors. Usually this is carried out as a contingency exercise to ensure that coverage for potential successors for key roles has been identified where none currently exists within an organisation. In the new gig economy, this process might be adapted so that strategic partners work together to capture the nebulous resource pool, by moving people around a collection of organisations in which they might fit. Some large corporates and government departments have been experimenting with this by seconding individuals to partner businesses and agreeing 'talent swaps'. This could be adapted as a concept by smaller more agile businesses. In particular, businesses that are growing rapidly, and where the experience and confidence of senior leaders may be outpaced by the growth of the business. These organisations may benefit from such talent swaps, perhaps with suppliers or trusted customers.

Top Tips:

+ Sponsorship from the top is key.

+ Be clear about goals, roles and processes.

+ Decide on open or closed membership according to the organisation's values.

+ Manage expectations and behaviours to avoid elitist divisions.

+ Make membership optional and flexible.

CHAPTER 7

MEASURING TALENT

Once a pool of high potential individuals has been identified, the next step is to use some method of objective measurement that will allow the talent pool to be reviewed and if necessary validated. This may be done before or after membership of the talent pool has been confirmed, as mentioned in the previous chapter. This will help to calibrate the performance and potential ratings of the nominees. Often this takes the form of a formal assessment. Depending upon their seniority and what the information will be used for, this may vary from one-to-one executive assessments through to an assessment centre. In most cases delegates are exposed to a series of tests that will assess their relative expertise against the yard stick that the business has agreed is what 'good' looks like.

An application process might be a useful strategy to adopt in those organisations where the talent may be outside the true employment boundaries. In this case, it would be critical to understand enough about the people who want to work for you, or don't want to work directly for you, but have key skills that you need, in order to understand where they might fit.

To ensure that the measurement is robust, the British Psychology Society (BPS) recommends you should map each of the identified knowledge, skills and behaviours onto at least two ways of measuring them. This is done so that there is always primary and secondary evidence that can be called upon to justify a decision. This improves the probability that the measures will accurately assess what the organisation wants to measure and will improve the chances of a decision being accurate. The graph below shows a typical mapping exercise for a role.

Mapping Criteria Exercise

	Interview	Role play	Group exercise		
Interpersonal sensitivity		1	1		
Written skills		1	2		
Knowledge of kite flying	1		2		

This critical step not only allows the business to ensure that all of the identified criteria for success have been identified but it also provides a template for weighting the evidence. This means that if there is a split vote, decisions have already been made about which of these data sets is most reliable. Inevitably there will be some who point out that even these methods are not foolproof and that bias and inaccurately applied criteria may not be robust. This is true. The most that can be claimed for these methods is that they improve reliability of an accurate decision beyond just the views of a manager. But they are not foolproof and should not be regarded as such. This is why any psychometric testing must always be followed by a discussion about results, so that their validity can be checked.

In the case of senior level delegates, in depth one–to–one with an external consultant, possibly after using some sort of personality questionnaires, can be very helpful. An in-depth report detailing the candidates' strengths and weaknesses to determine the relative merits of the individuals is produced after the interview. It will also highlight areas for development. In all cases, a report would be shared with the delegate before it is passed on, and feedback should be routinely offered, regardless of the outcome. This gives the candidate an opportunity to explain their results and sometimes this can be crucial.

Example:

A finance director scored quite badly on a psychometric test which was measuring her numerical reasoning for a development programme she had been invited to attend. During the debrief with the psychologist she revealed that during the test, which she had been doing in her office late at night, her boss had come in and started to ask her about the financial results of the business. It was a timed test and she could not stop it. She told her boss what she was doing, got him the results, and carried on with the test, still completing it in time. She knew that she was highly numerate, so had not mentioned it to anyone at the time as she believed that she had done quite well. However, she had missed some of the questions in her hurry and so the results were not as good as they should have been. She re-did the test and scored as highly as she had anticipated.

Assessment centres

In more junior roles, an assessment centre may be deployed for recruitment, promotion or entry onto a development programme. Exercises are used that have been mapped onto the job roles as closely as possible, so that they are representative of what a candidate would need to do. This allows assessors to more accurately identify how the individual operates in that specific role. Again, in all cases a report would be produced for discussion with the delegate and feedback offered regardless of the outcome.

The strength of this approach is that it allows all delegates to be measured on an even playing field. Using external assessors can give an objectivity and legitimacy to the process which can be very helpful in challenging group think and in defending decisions if questioned.

Interestingly, the case against using them is strong. Despite early research that indicated that they were effective, recent studies indicate that they are less predictive than expected[19]. In some cases using a single personality test that measures a personality factor called 'conscientiousness' is equivalent in effectiveness[20] to an assessment centre with a battery of tests.

And yet assessment centres continue to be used extensively in organisations because "they just seem to work". In other words, they have high face validity. Research[21] also suggests that assessment centres are still widely used, despite their huge cost, because there is a perception that they are 'felt fair' by all participants. This is an important consideration in organisations where the hiring or identification of talent needs to be something that the rest of the population buys into.

So how can assessment centres be improved? Recent research[22] has shown that the 'wash up' session favoured by many organisations as a way to calibrate results worsens their effectiveness in their ability to predict results. By just using the arithmetic scores from tests conducted improves the ability to predict future performance. Research suggests that the explanation for this might be due to a number of factors, for example group think, in which the 'wash up' meeting attendees begin to change, or confirm more strongly, and in this way results can become skewed. This skewing of results may become more pronounced when different levels of seniority play out in the room. One suggested process improvement might be to not hold a 'wash up' session to discuss the results but to accept the arithmetical scores as they stand. This remains unlikely to happen, because the appeal of post-consensus discussions is the perceived opportunity to overcome individual differences in biases (stringency/leniency) which may exist in other selection and assessment methods, when judgment relies on just one assessor, e.g. interview.

What accounts for the continued use of assessment centres? We know that training of assessors, use of multiple tests and multiple assessors are all recommended by the BPS, because research has shown that a combination of results will improve the predictive validity of the tests on their own. One of the best combinations is bio data and cognitive ability tests. Thus, assessment centres may appeal to many, as an opportunity to reach a perceived "fairer", more accurate, rating. It may also be that the ideas covered in an earlier chapter are also evident here. Managers taking part in an assessment centre may not be aware of the future direction of the business. Whilst they are fully able to assess the candidate against the current role, sometimes they are not willing or able to see past that current fit to the future needs of the business.

Which psychometric test to use where?

If the decision is reached that psychometric tests should be used, then the question of which one to use often crops up when organisations are trying to improve their conversion rate for applicants to those successfully appointed. The best advice is to ask an impartial expert. The British Psychology Society (BPS) should always be the first port of call because they are able to provide free substantive advice. They have a sub group called The Psychometric Forum who are able to help. Unfortunately, going to a test publisher, or even a test qualified practitioner, is likely to result in the test that the publishing house produces, or that which the expert is accredited in, being recommended. This can have disastrous consequences for all concerned, as using the wrong test for a particular situation will waste money and achieve the wrong result for all concerned.

As we have already seen, these tests are powerful and are used to discriminate between people, so using the right one is critical. There are some that are best suited to selection and there are others that should only ever be used in development. They are not necessarily interchangeable. It is critical to stay with the recommended use of a test if you want to stay out of jail!

If a test has been properly constructed, then it will be able to demonstrate the validity (i.e. how much it is likely to be able to measure what it says it will measure) and predictive scores (i.e. how reliable it is at measuring the same thing over a period of time, or different sample groups) which will show its worth. If you need to develop a test that is bespoke, then you will need a qualified occupational psychologist who has experience of test construction, but this is likely to be costly and time consuming.

Using a professionally developed test allows organisations to defend decisions. This is particularly important in relation to claims at an employment tribunal that a decision was biased. So, if an organisation is going to use a selection test for recruitment, promotion, entry into a talent pool, or onto a development programme, or anything that will infer an advantage to the person being 'selected' over those who are not, then it is much safer for organisations to use a valid test that has been professionally produced and externally validated. Using your own tests is problematic; consulting an expert is the safest way to mitigate that risk.

Hypothetical talent finding and non obvious moves

One scenario where involving current line managers in the talent process to identify potential may not be an option is where the future needs of the business are very different from the current operation. In this situation, the manager may simply not be in the know about the future strategic direction, may vehemently disagree with that direction, or the direction may have significant implications for the manager that are, as yet, unresolved. In this situation, the talent review may need to take place without managers being present.

In these circumstances, information may be produced that will be hypothetically based on 'what if' scenario planning and may not include current employees at all. The normal templates used by a business can be populated with both internal and external candidates, who may, or may not, be known to the business. In this case search consultants are sometimes retained to provide market mapping data that will give a business a view of the current incumbents of similar roles in different companies. Some of these businesses may be similar to the company that is looking, but in other cases they may use 'wild cards'. Internal candidates may be lined up on the basis of non-obvious moves, i.e. candidates who have no background in this area but show potential and could learn, given the right development and enough time in advance of the move happening.

Non-obvious moves are a great way to introduce challenge and diversity into a business. By considering non obvious candidates both internally and externally, a business can break free of its current make up and shake things up. As already mentioned, it can also be a way to incorporate gig economy workers who fall outside the normal employment relationship.

Example:

In an IT company a new service director needed to be appointed. The role was offered to and accepted by the finance director, who went on to do a fabulous job. He had already proven himself to be a great people manager, but he also understood the very complex warranty issues that had plagued this part of the business and had proved to be the undoing of the previous service director. The business benefited because it had continuity of cover, with someone already well versed in the business and a known quantity. The finance director benefitted because he was bored and had been discussing next moves with his boss, and had been exploring other options including leaving the business. This non obvious move was a great success for all concerned as it retained a key player in a growing business and gave him a breadth of experience to prepare him for even more senior roles in the future.

Although positive discrimination is illegal in the UK, positive action can be used highly effectively to address imbalances in a business. This means that identifying changes in the business and forecasting far enough out, allows organisations to introduce programmes such as 'He for She' positive action that allows businesses to think about a future role in a different way. Campaigns, such as this one, are actively approaching male leaders to enlist their help in addressing gender bias by acting as a role model for change. They can plan for future short lists to be more representative and balanced by helping under-represented groups to prepare for consideration when the time comes.

> **Example:**
>
> A well-known and highly regarded scientific establishment was set up by the government to conduct research in a particular field. As a condition of its funding it has been required to set up an educational outreach programme to encourage children to pursue scientific careers. As seen in STEM work, there is a worryingly under represented proportion of girls doing these subjects and so it was agreed that, as an extension of this programme, this establishment would launch a mentoring programme that takes female scientists from the business and sends them into schools where they are specifically targeting young girls to take scientific subjects at school. This has resulted in more girls gaining the right qualifications to allow them to apply for work and be considered by the organisation in the recruitment process. The recruitment process is a level playing field and the girls are not favoured in any way during the process, as this would constitute illegal discrimination. But is has increased the number of applications from girls for traditionally non-female roles.

Focus on the role

At their heart talent processes are designed to manage and anticipate risk. When the people being considered by the talent process have been reviewed, the next step is to consider the roles to be filled. By taking key roles in turn and identifying the gaps and overlaps, it quickly becomes clear where work needs to be done. In organisations where this has never been attempted, the business can get quite a shock at how underprepared it is to cover key roles. In addition, it will help to identify where key development needs to be targeted.

What sometimes happens is that talent data or 'pipelines' (e.g. data about people who may be able to progress to the next level) are drawn up by managers who populate them with unsuitable individuals. These candidates may be identified because they happen to be available and have always been thought of as the 'natural successor', or are individuals who are highly talented, so have been identified as successors in too many key roles. In both these cases the risk to the business is very high. The first scenario leads to a situation in which a vacancy occurs. Talent candidates who have been promised the next promotion are put forward, and they then become demoralised, or leave, when it doesn't happen and they fail to get the job. This leads to even more turnover and a greater dip in morale. The second scenario leads to a situation in which the identified successor has already been approached or, even worse, poached by one of the other many departments who saw him as a successor. So everyone begins an internal bidding war, driving up the cost of the candidate within the same organisation, increasing cost and reducing margin.

To avoid this happening, talent pipelines need to be developed that are honest, robust and joined up. Software exists that will allow companies to identify succession pipelines and some of these have now developed a capability to identify where a successor is being 'over used' by too many different departments and will highlight this as a risk. '81 boxes' is one such package, it is accessible on the internet and is a great example of what is available.

Top Tips:

+ Use the right test for the job. If in doubt ask a qualified expert.

+ Use hypothetical market mapping and non-obvious moves to challenge the status quo and handle the gig economy challenge.

+ Manage risk carefully; avoid being over dependent on one or two key candidates.

+ Consider positive action to increase the pool of candidates for roles with limited or scarce numbers, or where the balance of diversity is too heavily weighted in one direction.

+ Use technology software to help highlight gaps and overlaps.

CHAPTER 8

GROWING TALENT

A recent McKinsey article[23] estimated that US companies spend $14 billion annually on leadership development. They stated that 500 plus executives rank leadership development as one of their current and future priorities, yet only 7% of senior managers in the UK think that their companies develop global leaders effectively. They cited four reasons why leadership development fails:

1. Overlooking context

2. Decoupling reflection from real work

3. Under-estimating mind-sets

4. Failing to measure results

Much has been made of these four very straightforward lessons, and this chapter will help to provide guidance on how the lessons learned can be put into practice to improve the likelihood of success for talent interventions that will grow the talent in an organisation.

The word 'intervention' rather than programme is important here because applying the 70:20:10 rule plays an important part in tailoring the intervention to the most beneficial outcome for both the organisation as well as the employee. Growing talent is not always about running a programme. There are a myriad of ways in which development can take place, and the 70:20:10 model was developed to emphasise the fact that development takes place in many different forms. The model suggests that ideally an individual or an organisation should seek a balance of development formats that is made up as follows: 70% of development is gained through experience, 20% through individual interaction, coaching or feedback, and 10% through formal training.

70:20:10

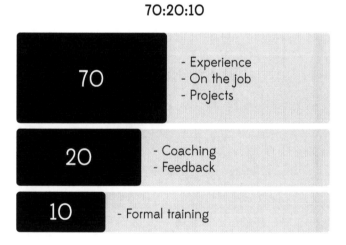

70 — Experience, On the job, Projects

20 — Coaching, Feedback

10 — Formal training

However, in their article '70:20:10: Where Is the Evidence?' Andrew Jefferson and Roy Pollock[24] suggest that it is unclear where the research evidence for this equation came from and that it is not necessarily a well-founded formula. They believe that it most likely came from work by McCall, Lombardo and Morrison[25] who were investigating elements of executive success. They asked 191 successful executives to respond to some version of the following question:

"Please identify at least three key events in your career, things that made a difference in the way you manage now. 1) What happened? 2) What did you learn from it (for better or worse)?"

Lombardo and Eichinger later summarised their findings in the *Career Architect Planner*[26] as follows:

Lessons learned by successful and effective managers are roughly:

- 70 percent from tough jobs

- 20 percent from people (mostly the boss)

- 10 percent from courses and reading.

However they go on to state that further research[27] recently went in search of the origins of the 70:20:10 rule and concluded that there is a lack of empirical evidence to support the model. It is unclear what the exact formula might be, and it appears that the basis for the proportions is less than precise. And yet it still provides us with a useful reminder that a mixture of different approaches and learning styles can be beneficial, if only to accommodate individual preferences in the learning population.

Context – what is the business imperative?

Any intervention should begin with the question, 'What is the problem we are trying to solve?' If you don't know the answer to this question, then it will be impossible to create a meaningful development intervention. In the same way that the chapter on 'talent finding' identified the need for the talent strategy to be an integral part of the business strategy, the same is true of the way in which a business chooses to 'grow' its talent.

Training Needs Analysis

If there is clarity about what is needed to deliver on the business outcomes, and the measurement of what already exists has taken place, then the business of growth becomes more straightforward. Where many businesses go wrong is that they assume that the same development is needed across the business and this is not necessarily the case. Imagine being in a class room where all of the lessons are being delivered at the pace of the slowest learner and aimed at the lowest level of capability. This would disengage most students. The same is true the other way around, where too much prior knowledge or capability has been assumed. Talent development programmes that sheep dip everyone through the same material are in fact communication vehicles for the business to bring their employees up to speed with certain things and can be very effective, if that is what they are intended to do. There are a huge number of tools that can be used to conduct a Training Needs Analysis, but essentially the formula is to identify the desired future state and measure the current level of capability. This can be done through many forms of data collection; observation, sampling, or questionnaires are often used. Sometimes it is sufficient to know that the training programmes are going to be used as a way to change the culture in some way. Then the same messages can be rolled out universally, with a bare minimum of data collection about what already exists in knowledge, skills and behaviour.

> **Example:**
>
> In a telecommunications company a change programme was introduced that was aimed at young leaders who could change the culture in the business to address the perceived threat from competitors in the same field. Launched and publicly led by the senior team, the roll out of this programme was considered to be hugely successful as it communicated a message about the reason for the change, galvanised action and provided the skills for participants to understand not only what they had to do, but how to make it happen. The programme had very clear deliverables and change occurred because the top team was consistently requesting feedback on the achievement of these deliverables. The sheep dip approach favoured by the development team on this occasion helped the programme to succeed because the learning that was acquired during the programme was able to be applied back in the workplace because the conditions had been set. Everyone had either just been, or were on, or were just going to attend the programme, so back in the work place everyone understood and were very positive about the changes being introduced.

This type of programme will be appropriate for some subjects, where a knowledge of legislation or new practices is required, an organisation culture change is needed, or where low levels of experience exist. But it will rarely be the right vehicle to develop individuals at more senior levels.

The first step in addressing the development needs of the business is to be really clear not only on the technical and business skills that are needed now and in the future, but also about the values and behaviours that the business wants to see in their employees. This critical first step cannot be circumvented because without it the business is not able to say what it wants to be known for. The best way to develop these values is with the input and engagement of all those in the business. The CEO needs to lead this work and take an active part in encouraging their direct reports to lead the way. Without this sponsorship, values and behaviours become a corporate tick box exercise in which words appear on walls, but are not something evidenced in the way that people do business with customers, suppliers and each other. It is important that leaders are visibly seen to be role modelling their own development.

> **Example:**
>
> Chairman and CEO of PepsiCo, Indra Nooyi, suggests that CEOs who continue to develop themselves are likely to be more successful.

Designing interventions that fit with the business needs and deliver for employees is a continuous process and needs to provide a firm structure for all development activity, especially that of any talent interventions. One way to ensure that this works is to develop a holistic picture so that people can see the connection between the different talent programmes and how they support the mainstream leadership development programmes. Several different methods are used here. A popular way to do this is by considering the category of talent that the individual falls into and then considering suitable options for them.

Once it is clear what the values and behaviours look like, the next step is to measure how well employees, in particular leaders, are living the values. Translating the values into what the organisation expects from its leaders is vital. Using a 360 degree feedback tool, or something similar, will provide factual data on which to work. From this an individual development path can be developed that will help to bridge the gap between where the leader is now and where they want to be.

It can be particularly off-putting for organisations who provide development knowing that this might be a skill that the individual will take abroad or to a competitor. This is particularly true of professional firms, e.g. accountancy firms, where a great deal of money has been ploughed into development and then the annual merry-go-round of employees happens, usually just after they qualify. But in providing development you are more likely to hang on to the good ones.

Using real work

Using real work is a great way to test talent, as long as it is done in the right way, i.e. they are supported and not just left to sink or swim. Sometimes you will move someone into a much bigger or more difficult role deliberately to see what happens. It is critical not to lose sight here of what you are doing and why; try to acknowledge and, to a certain extent, protect those people, because it can be hard to shine when you have been handed a really difficult problem area. In poorly-constructed development initiatives there is a tendency to write–off the talented individual when the problem is not solved immediately, or in the way that senior leaders think it should have been done. This 'hero to zero' mentality is unhelpful and can result in losing good people, simply because a problem they are facing is intractable, but that's why they were given it in the first place. Labelling the opportunity can help; they are sometimes called 'Booster' or 'Acceleration' roles and individuals can be red ringed (salaries and bonuses are preserved), to make sure that they are not penalised for accepting a really tricky project or role, and allow the individual to continue to progress.

Using real-life scenarios can be a useful learning environment, if everyone is in the right mind set. International assignments and global working will provide different scenarios for the talented employee to experience and appreciate difference; it is unclear how people prepare for taking on a different mind set to become international[28]. Even when working with international teams, differences show up that point to the difficulties that may be encountered by simple misunderstanding of language.

Example:

In a newly-formed global team, a video conference ended abruptly when the person chairing the meeting thought that they had reached a surprisingly fast conclusion in that everyone had agreed to the proposal on the table. What the UK team had actually said was: "We are all nodding here", as it was late in the evening due to the time difference and they had been at work all day. The US team thought that they had agreed and wound up the call very hastily, pleased with themselves that they had gained agreement on a sticking point. It was only after the call had ended and they were all looking at each other in the UK trying to figure out what had happened when they received an email summarising the main points, and showing agreement on a point that they absolutely had not agreed. The team leader then had to call her counterpart in the US and arrange a follow-up call for the next day.

In this context, it was possible to go back and use this as a learning opportunity to reflect on what had happened and summarise this as follows: 'Don't assume things and try to use plain language. If things seem wrong, they probably are.'

Mind set shifts

Competing teams can be good for an organisation and, where it is well handled, can create great opportunities for learning to take place, in particular where a mind-set shift is involved that means that participants will need to see the world differently. This is particularly true where it involves somebody in the equation conceding, or losing gracefully, for the good of the overall business.

Some people are much more prepared to share what they know with others, but where this is associated in some way with their own personal reputation or remuneration, they are unlikely to share. In some extreme cases they may prefer failing rather than seeing the bigger picture.

> **Example:**
>
> Two teams from the same organisation were bidding against each other for a piece of work, forcing the price down to unsustainable levels. When the customer finally accepted the lowest proposal and went to shake hands, the winning team had to withdraw because the return on investment had become uneconomic. The customer was left without a supplier, so went back to the second choice, same company different team. But this team also had to withdraw for the same reason as the first. The work could not be delivered because there was absolutely no margin in it. The teams had become so fixated on beating each other that the competitive element had overtaken good business sense. The customer walked away with a very poor view of the brand and had to find yet another provider, a competitor of the first company. The original winning company lost revenue and market share.
>
> The two teams were driven out of two different divisions and the leaders of those divisions had been set targets and goals by the COO that set them in direct competition with one another, as a deliberate ploy. There was no check or balance on the organisation that allowed senior leaders to monitor when this was getting out of hand, and there was no unifying goal that would protect the interests of the customer, the reputation of the brand and overall market share. This tactic of setting teams against each other can be a useful tool, but it needs to be used carefully and sparingly and be managed by a senior leader. Tying senior executives' bonuses and salaries to beating each other is not productive.

Mind set shifts are an important component of business improvement. Being agile and fleet of foot can help a business stay viable. 'Failing fast'[29] and then moving on are how you can learn what does and doesn't work. Without this, you create a risk averse culture, which might be OK in a business where this is a suitable culture, but where it is not, it can be significantly damaging.

Example:

In a pharmaceutical company there was a need to increase the number of drug targets that were being developed, so a meeting was held to review current projects. All the experts in a particular field were brought together and asked to share their work. Unsurprisingly, they shared their greatest success stories. When they were challenged to talk about the projects that hadn't gone well, and what they had learnt from this, there was a stunned silence. The business had made it not OK to be wrong, combining this with an acceptance that scientists are rewarded for publishing research which had to be as correct as possible when going to print. This had led to a culture of risk aversion. Given that this was the R&D part of the business, the new product pipeline began to dry up and the business began to lose market share, as competitors were cashing in on their reluctance to take a chance.

The meeting changed that view, and once the business began examining failures and making it OK to experiment as a way of speeding up publication of papers by examining all evidence, the pipeline once again opened up.

Using customers and talent pools to hothouse ideas and thoughts about how to take products further, or create the next generation of product, anticipate obsolete timings and envisage new threats that would challenge the whole way of doing business, is a great way to develop talent and the business at the same time. But first you need to make it safe to present the ones that went wrong and celebrate the work and effort that has been achieved. It is helpful to make it fun to share problems with each other and extend problem solving or interest groups. Introducing interactive whiteboards and open space will enable teams worldwide to continue to work on problems 24/7. This type of social collaboration enables businesses to recoup investment in infrastructure and equipment costs more quickly.

Measuring results

Training delivery is inextricably linked to measuring the results, and so it is important to understand what is, and is not, changing in how learning takes place. Technology has impacted learning like many other aspects of business. This has led to the phenomenon of a workforce in which so called 'Digital Natives' and 'Digital Immigrants', labels coined by Prensky in 2011[30], co-exist. He states that Digital Natives are those who have been born and brought up with the new technology. They do not know, or comprehend, a world in which it does not exist. Digital Immigrants on the other hand are a different generation and were not brought up around technology and have had to learn the new language and processes. It is as if they had landed in a new country. They approach work and learning from a different mind-set. The evidence behind Prensky's work is not strong and yet the ideas have caught the popular imagination as organisations seek to take into consideration the different approaches taken by these two groups.

Research[31] suggests that there is no generational difference in the way that people learn. Demographic factors such as gender, mode of study (distance or place-based) and the international or home status of the student are equally important.

In the case of the younger generation, their exposure to technology appears to make them more familiar with the use of technology, but it does not make it a better medium for training delivery. This research suggests that the millennials have a familiarity with technology and enjoy ICT being used in moderation, but no gulf between teachers and learners has been found. Their work has shown that students still prefer to be taught in a way that suits their learning style. Other research[32] has found similar results. Their work points to the fact that the use of technology may vary between subjects; for example, engineering students broadly make more use of technology. But the researchers have suggested that this is because of their interest in technical subject matter per se, rather than a generational difference.

Nevertheless, it would be foolish to deny the very real impact that the changes in technology are having. It is changing business so rapidly that it is no longer possible to predict what will happen next. Change is now a constant and not changing is not an option. So how do businesses prepare to deliver training to their employees in a way that keeps up with these changes? Forward-thinking organisations like BT have employed teams of futurologists to help them to predict future trends. Leaders have always needed to be able to predict the future to a certain extent, but now they need to be able to imagine what might happen with high levels of ambiguity and uncertainty. Individuals may be moving faster than some companies.

Organisations such as Barclays have recognised that there is a schism occurring in the way that people operate and have answered this with the introduction of their Digital Eagles who assist people going into their banks and are now faced with a computer terminal rather than a cashier desk. They want to help customers to make the shift in interaction that the Bank needs them to make. It doesn't want to lose their custom, but it cannot continue to operate in the way that it has. This is certainly an example of an organisation that has decided to provide a way to help digital immigrants to bridge a gap. But it is NOT a reflection of technological training delivery. In fact, the opposite is true, as one-to-one teaching is at the heart of this method.

Training programmes have been repeatedly pointed at as being a thing of the past and yet they continue to survive. Technology such as open space, interactive whiteboards, gaming and even second life are being used as platforms to reach out and educate people, as the general public become more familiar with technology on an everyday basis. Yet, they are rarely the only form of training provided.

ROI – Training evaluation

To date, the most widely used model of training evaluation is that by Don Kirkpatrick[33] who developed the four level model, in which evaluation of training is measured through the following:

Kirkpatrick Model

At level one of Kirkpatrick's evaluation model – Reaction (to what degree a participant reacts to the training event), it might be argued that talent development achieves its objectives because it is generally high profile and accompanied by some type of career progression and a move of some sort. One might assume that this creates both excitement and some trepidation for those embarking on a programme, and this may mean that the learner is pre-disposed to feeling positive about any support that they receive. It does not necessarily mean that the training is effective.

Level two – Learning (to what extent a participant learns the knowledge, skills and abilities), and Level three – Behaviour (how much learners are able to apply what they have learned), relate to whether an organisation is able to absorb and assimilate the learner back into the workplace. Research suggests that the environment that the learner is returning to, relapse prevention and high job relevance are all intrinsically linked to the successful transfer of learning[34]. In other words, it is important for the organisation to be ready for the talent pool member to want to make changes and see these as valid. This can be achieved through preparation by an organisation to accept the learner back into the organisation, and interventions such as follow-ups and inter-session work, as well as great preparation to tailor the training to the relevant jobs, will all help to ensure that learning is effective.

One key question here is how to evaluate without creating an issue in the organisation. Does the business need to know that someone from their team has been developed on a talent programme and is expected to be different as a result? And if so, how will this change the dynamics within a team? All of this needs to be carefully thought through and may provide an answer to the earlier question as to whether membership of a talent pool should be overt or covert.

If the aim of talent development is to support Level four – Results, and achieve tangible results which might translate to acceleration of progression for the talent pool member, then one might assume that companies will routinely assess how far and how quickly talent pool members progress as a result of the programme of development. So it is important to track who has been placed where, and how quickly they progress after attending the programme. Whilst this is the intention of many talent teams, the reality is that a technical tracker needs to be used to help ensure that delegates are constantly 'on the radar'. Without it, data and tracking is lost.

Where the learning experience is closely linked to a significant business outcome then ROI is much easier to measure. This provides not only a more satisfying environment for the learner, who feels that they are learning on the job and proving their worth, but it can also provide huge benefit for the business. Where this is a financial payback, then this has a double benefit of also cost justifying the learning experience. In some organisations, talent programmes are connected to an expectation that the delegates will produce a new revenue stream, or save money for the business. Having a financial target attached to this can help the delegate to focus on those experiences that will enable them to learn and make money. In the following example millions of dollars were generated by this real life intervention.

Example:

A highly-talented team leader was managing a team that was working on a project to design a new product. It was just after a merger and the two cultures had not yet properly assimilated. The project team would come together, at great expense, from all around the world. They were trying to make a decision about the product and everyone would agree on the outcome during the meeting, but they would go back to their home country and gradually the phone calls would begin, with team members letting the team leader know one by one that they really could not agree to the decision that had been made. He couldn't work it out. It was a binary decision and shouldn't have been that difficult, but for some reason they couldn't find a solution that stuck.

Eventually he called in a coach and she interviewed each of the team members and then came back to him with her findings. It was clear that there was a total split in the team and that this was between the two different companies that had existed previously. The values of the two companies had been completely different, and one was interested in selling as many units as possible and the other was interested in product safety. This led to an inability to make a decision because they did not have a new agreement about criteria for decision making. Once this had become clear, it was obvious what the problem was and what was needed to resolve it.

They had one final meeting to discuss the product and the coach fed back the finding of her report. They were still applying old norms. As a newly-formed team, they had not created a new set of criteria to use for decision making. They set about doing that with the help of the coach and made the elusive decision. The members of the product team went their separate ways and the team leader had no phone calls. The product went to market ahead of the competition which meant that they could register for intellectual property rights, and it went on to make millions of dollars.

The lesson learned by the team leader was a valuable one: not to assume that teams that work together are all working with the same principles. You have to make goals, values and criteria explicit and known within the team, so that they can be debated in order to be accepted. It might appear to be quicker to avoid these conversations, but this will come back and bite you. It is particularly important when you have two different companies that have come together. You can't just stick them together and ignore their heritage and differences. You have to dissect the old to create new, carrying out an analysis of different beliefs, and work through a new set. It is not enough to look at this on a macro level, because sometimes senior managers are deluding themselves about how embedded the thinking is, and the only way to test this is by asking the questions at an individual level.

The revenue generated by the product more than compensated for the cost of the coach, and project teams were assigned coaches to improve productivity.

The next case study is an example of how a learning intervention can cost money and impact reputation if handled incorrectly.

Example:

A young graduate proposed an idea to change the way in which travel expenses were reimbursed. Those in a particular contract were given a car and a mileage allowance that allowed them to fill up with fuel to complete their business miles. Their jobs were entirely on the road. The decision was welcomed by the strategy director who was tasked with saving money, and a memo was issued to communicate the changes. After what can only be described as a near all-out strike, the student was asked to attend a discussion about the decision that he had proposed. It became apparent that he had only completed desk research and that the idea had been prompted by a friend who worked in a similar role for a large consulting firm in London. What he had failed to appreciate was that the decision to change the policy had a material effect on the lives of those affected. The policy saved money in the short term for the company, by passing the cost of travel directly to the workers who had no way of absorbing that cost. When challenged, he simply said that he believed that everyone has a credit card, not appreciating that many of the low-paid workers affected by this change did NOT have credit cards. They were balancing finely-tuned home cash flows around the ebb and flow of income and outgoings. Furthermore, the friend who had suggested it was dealing with a very different audience, higher paid, and in London, where the availability of public transport was much greater. Effectively what he had done was given all of these workers a pay cut and asked them to subsidise the company cost reductions. It cost the business tens of thousands of pounds to recover the situation, but the goodwill and trust of the people took much longer.

The lesson learned was to ensure that development programmes which place talent in the business to do a real job need to acknowledge the true skill and experience level of the delegate and the delegate needs to be monitored appropriately in the tasks that are assigned. Without support and back up, any talent placement can be highly risky for the business.

A useful way to support young talent is through the appointment of a mentor. Mentors differ from coaches in that they provide substantive input and advice based on their experience. Rather than a coach, who is there to support an individual to make their own choices through careful questioning, the right mentor will be able to share their experience and knowledge of how business works. A mentor is able to discuss ideas and give feedback on suggestions such as the one proposed by the graduate in the previous example, before it becomes a reality and, in this case, a serious issue.

Top Tips:

+ Role model from the top: the CEO should be demonstrating their learning.

+ Use a tool such as 360 degree feedback to give the individual insight and create a starting point to measure progress.

+ Use real work as opportunities to develop, making sure that the right support is in place.

+ Training needs analysis, and an appreciation of learning styles is important to consider when creating training design and delivery methods.

+ Don't assume that technology is the answer to training future generations.

CHAPTER 9

KEEPING TALENT

There are generally three reasons why you might lose talent that you want to keep:

1. They leave.

2. You no longer consider them to be talent, because they have stopped performing.

3. They no longer wish to be considered to be talent.

In essence, those individuals that an organisation wants to retain, but who have decided to leave, either physically, mentally, or emotionally. They are no longer 'engaged' in the success of the organisation. Much has been written about engagement, but until recently it was not entirely clear what it was, or how it could be achieved. In their seminal work, *Engaging for Success*, David MacLeod and Nita Clarke have found what they believe to be four pillars of engagement, namely:

- Strategic narrative

- Engaging managers

- Employee voice

- Integrity

They have shown that these four elements are present in highly successful organisations and are critical to keeping employees engaged, productive, healthy and willing to 'go the extra mile', regardless of whether they are talent or not.

But what is the evidence that MacLeod and Clarke are right, besides the numerous case studies of organisations which they cite as having been successful as a result of engagement?

From occupational psychology we learn that there are several well-researched theories which might support their findings. Research into motivation, performance management and the impact of rewards on behaviour all provide evidence that what they have found is indeed backed up by research evidence.

Motivation is generally considered to be what keeps people in an organisation, and persisting in their role. Yet it is a complex issue. Much has been written about the 'happy productive worker' and a great deal of research has been conducted, but the evidence for the relationship between satisfaction and performance remains unproven[35]. It would appear that happy workers are not necessarily more productive, but they are more likely to be engaged and want to stay. So retention of talent in your organisation may well rest on whether individuals are happy. Tapping into the right motivation for them is likely to be what will make the difference between whether they stay or go.

Strategic narrative – do I know what I am doing and why?

Having a mission statement helps an organisation to set the context for what it is trying to achieve. Many organisations have a goal that is very explicit in their mission statement, and it is generally translated into meaningful terms that all employees understand. This can help to focus work. Here are some examples:

Example:

Amazon.com: "It's our goal to be Earth's most customer-centric company, where customers can find and discover anything they might want to buy on line."

Coca-Cola: "To refresh the world in mind, body and spirit. To inspire moments of optimism and happiness through our brands and actions. To create value and make a difference."

Google: "Google's mission is to organise the world's information and make it universally accessible and useful."

Providing this context in a way that is accessible, easily understood and attractive to employees and customers alike is a crucial success factor in engaging employees and keeping them.

Engaging Manager – does my manager help me to perform?

Being an 'engaging manager' would seem to be relatively straightforward, and yet anecdotally it appears to be the most frequently cited reason why employees choose to leave.

So what can a manager do to be more engaging? There is an abundance of theories that managers might draw on to be more engaging, and a few are suggested below.

Expectancy Theory[36] basically states that people will do things if they expect to be rewarded appropriately, or 'fairly', for what they do. It has been the basis on which managers have manipulated pay and other benefits to be in line with the expectation of the employee, which works if the levels of pay are sufficient and match the expectations of an employee. However, it ignores habitual behaviour, subconscious motivation and spur-of-the-moment decisions. It also fails to identify that people can be motivated by ideals, principles and social obligations rather than pleasure. It makes an assumption that people are rational beings. Research suggests that it is better at predicting intentions than choices to actually perform[37]. Nevertheless, it does suggest that managers who do this well are likely to motivate their employees.

Equity theory[38] on the other hand is about motivation to outperform others. It suggests that people compare themselves to others and, if they believe themselves to be better than others but are not rewarded at the same, or better, level, they will take steps to redress the imbalance. Managers might use this theory when they set up league tables and competitions between teams that allow them to compare and contrast performance.

Goal setting theory[39] suggests that the majority of people are motivated to achieve a goal and that both motivation and job performance will be higher when four conditions are met:

- The goals are clear and specific

- The goals are difficult

- The goals are accepted

- Feedback is provided

This theory may have been the basis for the dominance of the SMART goals, favoured by many organisations, in which goals are set using the following Mnemonic:

S   pecific

M   easurable

A   chieveable

R   ealistic

T   imebound

So what is the evidence that Goal Setting Theory (GST) works[40]? A wealth of literature exists that suggests that GST is effective in an organisation. Much of this evidence has been based on what happens in laboratories, but there is a growing body of evidence to suggest that it is also effective in organisations. In businesses where goals are set at the beginning of the year and shared widely across the business, these are translated into objectives. They can be published so that everyone can see them on the intranet, providing they are not share price sensitive. People need to know where they are headed, and without this as a yard stick they can become deflated or lost, so providing feedback is fundamental to making sure that individuals continue to feel motivated. Colleagues understand what is being worked on and can offer support, feedback or even assistance to help others achieve their goals. Research[41] has shown that organisations that use goal setting theory have found that downtime on systems and time to resolve issues have all reduced because the whole organisation is aware of, and working on, problems that the business needs to overcome.

Engaging managers also take time to get to know their teams and will work with them to develop learning and development plans to help them to grow. All of these roles that a manager needs to fulfil are going to be important in retaining the right people in an organisation.

Employee voice – Do I have a say in what I am trying to achieve?

The theory shows that commitment to achieving the goal creates feelings of achievement, sense of closure and enhanced self-esteem and may also deliver on rewards (e.g. pay, recognition) which can have beneficial effects when these are valued by the employee.

Studies have shown that when goals are set that are specific and difficult (but not impossible) and when feedback is provided, performance is enhanced. This appears to be particularly true if the feedback is self-generated or provides immediate performance feedback[42]. This improvement in performance and feedback are likely to be contributing factors in motivating an individual and may play a crucial role in their intention to stay, although employee retention and intention to quit are highly complex areas in which opinion is divided.

Some research[43] has also shown that goal acceptance increases performance and that more difficult goals are chosen when an employee is involved in the process, although other researchers[44] have found that it may depend upon how 'acceptance' is defined. Nevertheless, involvement in the process of defining and agreeing goals that are set would appear to be important in some cases for the goal to be achieved and for it to motivate and retain employees.

Integrity – Do people I work with live the values?

Other behaviours such as teamwork, honesty, etc, are equally if not more important to how we measure people, and theories of motivation don't provide answers to this. The values that an organisation chooses to espouse and whether or not these are evident in how employees operate will be important. This can be reinforced and rewarded by organisations in various ways:

Example:

One IT organisation used a bi-annual bonus that was entirely discretionary and was awarded for exhibiting the right behaviours and living the values. This was in addition to, but separate from, achievement of objectives and goals, which were rewarded through salary increases in the normal way.

Is motivation changing?

Articles have recently been written about generational differences and to some extent gender differences. Whilst much of this evidence, as we have already seen, is yet to be proven, it is interesting to take it into consideration when reviewing how to keep talent in your organisation.

The HBR article, 'What Do Millennials Really Want at Work? The Same Things the Rest of Us Do', which we have already reviewed in the chapter relating to what attracts employees to an organisation, has already pointedly made the case that all generations would want the same thing.

The following provides some questions raised by the list and some practical solutions and options for how an organisation might deliver on these expressed needs, so that they are better able to motivate and retain their talent pool members.

1. The number one desire they have is to 'make a positive impact on my organisation'. The findings outlined in this paper do appear to be evidence based and provide an accurate insight into what makes people motivated, happy and want to stay

in an organisation. For example, one could argue that the desire to make a positive impact on an organisation could be rooted in Goal Setting Theory. But, if this is the case, how can new businesses, where the higher purpose is not very obvious, attract and retain employees when it is not obvious what they are doing yet? Just as Apple was the company that satisfied a need in us that we didn't know we had, then it is important to find a higher reason for the company's existence. As we have already seen, organisations tend to create a mission statement to co-exist with their values.

2. The second most important factor is cited as being able to 'help solve social and/or environmental challenges'. One could argue that this too is underpinned by Goal Setting Theory, as it is a goal that is self-directed and probably difficult to achieve.

3. The third most important factor is to work with a diverse group of people.

These factors may be what employees say that they want at work, but there is a specific area of study that has focused on 'happiness' that provides further evidence of the importance of social interaction. Albeit that there is not a great deal of evidence linking happiness to productivity, it is likely that happy workers will be more likely to stay in an organisation. A study in the British Medical Journal found that happiness in social networks may spread from person to person. Researchers followed nearly 5000 individuals for 20 years and found that happiness tended to spread through close relationships like friends, siblings, spouses and next-door neighbours; researchers reported that happiness spread more consistently than unhappiness through the network[45]. This tribalism, or sense of community, may be easy to achieve in a conventional organisation, but how does this work for those who are part of the gig economy? How do organisations that choose to regard these pools of non-employees as extensions of their talent cadre make them feel part of the business, and yet not draw them in too closely? Some organisations are now offering learning and development opportunities to those outside their business and even their industry as a way to engage with those who are not directly employed by them. Innovation in the way that organisations approach this problem is very welcome. Some outstanding work is being done, in particular in the financial sector, where organisations are offering 'returnships' © Morgan Stanley, or intern programmes of a set number of weeks to reintroduce non-employee maternity returners to the workplace and improve their diversity balance. But what more can be done to satisfy this employee desire?

4. 'Work for an organisation among the best in my industry', is the fourth factor highlighted as being important to employees. Research[46] has shown that reputation has a significant impact on an employee's desire to join or stay with a company. It may also play an increasingly important role in attracting non-employees to work with the company and offer their expertise.

5. & 6. 'Do work I am passionate about' and 'Become an expert in my field' seem to relate to interest in the subject and a desire to learn. There is a plethora of research that looks at what makes people happy, self-esteem and learning preferences. Again, research in the British Medical Journal[47] has found that Sociometric status, (i.e. the amount of respect one has from face-to-face peer group) is significantly and causally related to happiness as measured by subjective well-being. Self-determination[48] theory is another school of thought which relates to an individual's need for competence, autonomy and relationships with others and may be of importance for those interested in retaining talent. Results show that these needs are very important to well-being and performance. Organisations might respond by offering appropriate training and development and allowing the individual to work in areas of choice to enhance their sense of competence. In some technology businesses, it is standard practice to give employees

a certain degree of latitude to work on projects in which they have a deep interest alongside the targeted objectives of their teams, and this gives them a sense of autonomy and freedom. One could argue the gig economy workers are already well placed in this regard and it is hard to know how an organisation to which they are connected might contribute, aside from offering development as it occurs. The final need, that of relationships, is likely to be governed by the values and behaviours exhibited by those in an organisation.

7. 'Manage my work-life balance' has been well practiced in many organisations, although, as has already been mentioned, there now appears to be a trend for flexibility on location to be retracted. Organisations looking to retain talent may be well advised to consider maintaining and even extending flexible working, if this is what employees are saying that they want. One practical solution to retaining talent, but introducing greater freedom of movement, is using study leave and sabbaticals. They can be a great way to retain and continually develop employees and, if necessary, can reduce or contain costs. People would rather have unpaid leave and take time off to study, travel or spend time with family than anything else. Parental leave coaching and / or coaching for elderly dependants can also enhance and underline an organisation's commitment to flexible working in a very tangible way.

Example:

One FTSE 100 company runs various talent programmes that have been mapped on to each other, so that they can see how people are progressing. On a regular basis they look at diversity. As a result of looking at what the stats were saying, they introduced a maternity and paternity coaching programme. This has helped them to increase the number of people returning from parental leave from 25% to 100% over a one-year period.

They employed a company that also provides elderly dependance care. They held a view that one of the reasons that women don't reach senior roles in companies is that they become overwhelmed by their family responsibilities at the same time that they would normally be stepping up to a more senior role. The programme allows the company to support them to bridge the gap between holding down a demanding job and taking care of elderly parents and/or children. They have seen huge improvements, more so with women than with men.

The scheme is offered to all employees, and the vast majority of people taking it up are women, but some men have also used it.

---

8. & 9 'Become a senior leader' and 'Achieve financial security' are often connected. The wish to become more senior is often connected with a wish to increase rewards. Contrary to popular opinion, there is a lack of evidence that money doesn't motivate. In the past a great deal of research has focused primarily on negative aspects of extrinsic motivation or rewards. For example, research has demonstrated that intrinsically motivated activities, i.e. things that we do because we want to do them not because we are expecting a reward, promote feelings of competence and independence, whereas being offered a reward can undermine these feelings[49]. Conclusions have been drawn that rewards undermine performance, but research shows that this is not necessarily the case[50]. It may

depend upon who is setting the reward. In particular, the impact of money has attracted a huge amount of attention and has been shown to decrease performance[51], leading to a view that extrinsic motivation does not motivate. Other research has countered this, showing that where 'piece rate' is raised to a high enough level for this to be meaningful, it DOES motivate the person being paid[52].

Other researchers[53] have shown that 'owning' the reward may mean that it is possible for motivation to avoid being undermined. Neuroscientists have found recently that rewards can have a positive effect on attention and memory, and they argue that, if the right goals can be found, they will actually enhance performance[54].

It is a commonly held view that money doesn't motivate. However, as we have already seen, research doesn't quite say that. It says that the right level of reward appropriately shaped and selected by the individual DOES motivate. This means that employees need to be able to choose their rewards. Salary sacrifice systems work in this way, and where they have been introduced they are popular. But not everyone wants the same thing; for example, in some scientific research roles it is more important to employees to be first author on a research paper because of the kudos that this generates. One way around this is to ask employees what they want to have as a reward and tailor salary sacrifice schemes to their needs as well as that of the business.

It is hard to imagine how organisations might accommodate these needs for those in the gig economy, apart from to pay well and on time!

10. 'Start my own business' was the final driver identified and clearly many of those who are in the gig economy already have the advantage. But how can organisations motivate and inspire their internal talent with such a desire. The first thing to say is

that this is not going to be all of the population. The second thing is that many organisations have the opportunity to help their employees to feel as if the place where they work is akin to being an owner.

In summary, it seems that whilst there are some differences in what generations want, the similarities are far greater because the fundamental building blocks of motivation are the same. Setting goals that are agreed with the employee, providing regular feedback and ensuring that people know and understand what they will get if they achieve their goals, appears to work. It is the principle on which most good appraisal systems have been based and have been highly successful. Whilst it may be true that some of these appraisal systems are ineffective, from what we understand from the research, it is unlikely that human nature has changed substantially and more likely that the appraisal processes that have been introduced in business and operated over many years may not be being used very effectively, and it is this that has caused there to be a break down in trust and confidence in appraisals. Whilst we like to think that there are some universal constructs, evidence suggests that it is much more nuanced. What motivates one person may actually demotivate another. This can make it really difficult for line managers who are trying to figure out what they need to do to keep the individual players and the entire team on side, both to achieve short-term goals and to retain talent on a long-term basis.

Top Tips:

+ Motivation hasn't really changed, so improve but don't change appraisals.

+ Not having a performance rating will impact how you manage the talent assessment process.

+ Flexibility of working times and location is a double-edged sword.

+ Pay and rewards can be effective in motivating if they are self-selected by the employee and set at the right level.

CHAPTER 10

REPLACING TALENT

There will always be some roles, in particular ones that need scarce technical capability, where it is difficult to plan for succession. But where it is possible to do so, particularly in some key leadership roles, developing a heat map will help to identify where 'flight risks' (likelihood of leaving the company in a given timescale showing succession coverage) for key candidates exist, or where an organisational exposure might occur.

A heat map is a pictorial image of the flight risk (i.e. the likelihood of that person leaving), as it relates to a key role:

Heat Map for flight risks

ROLE	6 – 12 months	1 – 2 years	2+ years
Managing Director	X	✓	✓
Operations Director	✓✓	✓✓	X

X = No Successors identified   ✓ = 1 Successor identified   ✓✓ = 2 + Successors identified

This can be constructed relatively easily following conversations with the individual about their aspirations and, where possible, timescales that they are using for the next step. The heat maps need to be actively monitored on a regular basis both formally and informally. They can also highlight and manage risk around exposure when key roles are vacant.

Where businesses are changing rapidly, managing flight risks becomes more important and yet ironically also more difficult and critical. It can become so challenging that some organisations simply give up and refuse to do it. In some situations, this might be the right thing to do. But in the majority of businesses a contingency plan is usually going to be helpful, even if it simply highlights the issue.

Meeting with key talent in an organisation on a regular basis, to discuss their career aspirations and where possible next moves might take them, is an effective way to anchor people into a business. A note of caution here is to avoid over promising opportunities that cannot be delivered as this will have a negative effect. Equally, delivering next moves can create an 'expectancy' mentality if not managed appropriately. Using an external coach as a sounding board can provide advice, guidance and skills for the individual to take the next step for themselves, without promising anything inappropriate.

Changes in the psychological contract

Changes in the way in which people run organisations is calling into question how the psychological contract has worked and should work in the future. By that I mean, what is the nature of the relationship between employee and employer, when the contract is short term, flexible, temporary or a contract for services rather than employment? Organisations are being forced to reconsider how they engage and develop employees with non-standard careers alongside traditional workforces[55]. But very little has been discussed or written about how this might impact the talent agenda. The psychological contract and expectations of the myriad of different workers need to be re-examined and addressed in potentially different ways, without disadvantaging either party[56]. There is evidence to suggest that providing training for contingent workers may help to build commitment[57], but there are employment law implications which must be considered to avoid an employment contract relationship being inferred, and this would be the same with any other material support provided by an employer. Perhaps it is time for these laws to be questioned and changed?

Research has attempted to provide new labels, but there has been a great deal of criticism levelled at the 'boundaryless' and 'protean' careers, that they are imprecise in their definitions. Do they refer to individuals who move between organisations? Or individuals who refuse roles and promotions because of external concerns? Does boundaryless working over-emphasise individual employees and performance which may undermine teamwork? This might lead an organisation to question how and whether it should support this type of working. The remit of the talent agenda is being opened up beyond the scope of the organisation, to perhaps encompass the sector in which it operates. Are organisations supposed to collaborate or compete on this basis? It would appear that some are now competing in how well they collaborate. All of this makes an assumption that an organisation would wish, and would be able, to support careers both non-standard and traditional. There are several arguments to be made against this occurring.

To date, research and theory has concentrated on a Western interpretation of careers. Plenty of evidence exists to support the view that 'careers' are socially constructed[58]. In order for a global organisation to provide career support, in both traditional and non-standard ways, it will have to develop a thorough understanding of the cultural differences impacting individuals and accommodate this. Individual employees rather than organisations may be the ones who dictate what will happen as they follow career paths which may include such things as self-initiated expatriation (SIE) careers. We are seeing this in the rise of phenomena such as 'Corporate Nomads' who select work and move around the world in order to experience travel and be exposed to different cultures.

Organisations may be grappling with how to 'retain' or replace those employees who are pursuing non-standard careers (perhaps they are seeking international assignments or freedom to set up their own business). Tension occurs where these individuals may be those that organisations seek to retain as scarce and valuable assets[59]. By offering international secondments and internal moves to attract and retain those with core skills because this is what they inherently seek[60], organisations may then exacerbate their own issues in trying and failing to retain core capabilities when and where they are needed by the organisation, rather than where the employee wants to be working[61].

People may only pursue work that they believe they can do. So they may be inhibited or emboldened to pursue a career, based rightly or wrongly, on their own view of their capability. Research in this area[62] has shown that self-belief is critical to make a success of a new career. In other words, if you believe that you can, you will. If you don't believe that you can, you won't. If an organisation wants to encourage those who do not work for them to believe that it is possible for them to join their organisation and follow a particular career path, then they may need to consider how they instil confidence that an individual can still achieve their aims of being self-employed and yet employed by an organisation that wants to retain them.

One way in which it might be helpful for organisations to consider how they replace those leaving their organisation, or their industry, is to examine different models of career development so that they can consider how joining them may fit into someone's career pattern. One such model is the career construction – life design theory[63]. It is a theory in which the employee re-examines their life in the context of skills that they can bring to their new employment. This may be useful for organisations and individuals where the workforce is constantly leaving or entering work, for example where women are returning to work after breaks to care for children or elderly dependants and need to develop a sense of who they are as a professional, as distinct from being a mother [64]. By using this model, organisations can help women who have been out of the workforce for some years to redefine the skills and capabilities that they used in the home and understand how these might apply in the workplace. This life design technique might be offered by career counselling and could be applied to both those who pursue a traditional and a non-standard career. This might have particular application where a major life event has taken place, for example, expatriation or return from work for those who have been long-term absent. We are already beginning to see this being applied in the government-funded returners engagement programmes offered by companies and organisations aiming to encourage women back into the workplace.

Another career development structure that might be considered is[65] the life span careers theory which encompasses other roles outside work and provides a reference point for individuals to consider their wider life as equally and, at times, more important elements of their existence[66]. Extensions of this life span theory have resulted in Kaleidoscope Career patterns[67] which recognise the way in which people's careers, in particular women's, move in and out of prominence according to the other things that are happening in their lives, and the growing assumption that dual career paths will be the norm[68].

For organisations this recognition of different needs and priorities occurring over time will be critical for replacing workers who experience altering needs during their employment life cycle. Matching benefits such as flexible working and retirement wind-downs to the experiences of employees, in particular with the core traditional employees, may be key to future talent retention.

Top Tips:

+ Reconsidering the talent agenda in the light of changes in what people want from work.

+ Developing and maintaining a heat map to manage risk.

+ Understanding what 'talent' wants is part of an ongoing regular dialogue.

+ Re-think how you engage with those outside the business.

+ Supporting non-traditional careers through the psychological contract.

CHAPTER 11

LEADERSHIP

What do businesses want from their leaders?

Thousands of articles have been written that have attempted to define what a leader is. None of the answers have been universally accepted, but two schools of thought have emerged. The first is the 'Great Man' theory (funnily enough, not a Great Woman theory!), which suggests that leadership characteristics are what can be identified and developed in different individuals. Originally, the concept was based on a view that a few privileged individuals were born to be leaders and that they could not be made. The second school of thought is that leadership is a process and that followers and leaders hold and use different roles in relation to power.

In 1981 the American Management Association commissioned McBer consultant Richard Boyatzis to examine whether a generic model of managerial competency could be derived from various individual competency models. As a result of his research, Boyatzis listed 19 generic management competencies in his book *The Competent Manager* published in 1982. This list has never been accepted universally and most organisations persist in developing their own bespoke definition, claiming that the role or the practice of leadership in their particular organisation is very different. This seems to be driven out of a desire to go beyond the competition and create something that is better and more fitted to excellence in their market place. But it is also true that the cost of creating a bespoke version for an organisation may well outweigh the benefits.

A typical example of the identification of characteristics and skills is the report from the ILM[69] which revealed areas that were done badly by leaders in the opinion of their followers and then contrasted this with what the leaders stated was their focus for development. The report highlighted that there was a difference between the two lists, suggesting that leaders did not necessarily have an accurate view of how their followers saw them.

A practical tool that helps to overcome this would be to use a reputable 360 degree questionnaire such as The Leadership Practices Inventory (LPI) by Kouzes and Posner[70]. It is behavioural based, well researched and easy to use. It allows individuals to request feedback from others on how the leader performs. As a starting point, it is a great way for organisations who do not have the time, inclination or money to develop their own bespoke model to use an off-the-shelf tool to baseline leadership practices against the following five behaviours:

- Challenging the process

- Inspiring a shared vision

- Enabling others to act

- Modelling the way

- Encouraging the heart

Measuring these five common behaviours provides great evidence for the individual not only to understand how others think they operate, but how they could be even better at being a leader. It is easily mapped onto most organisation values and can be a quick and easy way for businesses to begin work in this area.

However, the main challenge of this report, and to a certain extent the LPI, is that it seems to reflect what is required by leaders today and does not necessarily take into consideration what might be needed in the future by leaders. Indeed this anticipation of what future 'leader-like' qualities might be is the subject of a great deal of continuous speculation.

Organisations are becoming increasingly diffuse and unrecognisable as one entity, which means that the role of leadership becomes harder for one person to learn to do. As businesses change, so the role of a leader changes and will keep changing, and those who are agile and can reinvent themselves, or flex their style according to the situation they are facing, will be amongst the most successful.

Different organisations, business sectors, development cycles and customer bases need different skills and different approaches at different times. Venture capitalists know that the entrepreneur who starts a business is rarely the right person to continue to run it in steady state. But introducing different and challenging leadership to an organisation can be incredibly difficult to achieve successfully. How frequently does an organisation build 'future difference' into its senior hiring programme, to then find that the candidate they have hired leaves the business very quickly because the culture of the organisation is too strong and rejects them? This seems to happen with great regularity in football clubs that expel the 'unsuccessful' leader who has been unable to change the team and lead it to success. The question is whether the team or the leader was the right choice to keep?

Perhaps it is time for us to see leaders through a different lens. It seems that the growth of the gig economy has created a growing tribe of 'Organisational Nomads', freelance, interim, self-employed workers who move between and within organisations. This may call for leaders who can inspire and engage a peripatetic workforce. To date, research into leadership of a nomadic workforce has been lacking and what little has been done has focused on systems and technology-enabled working[71]. But we also know that in most nomadic tribes there is a culture of storytelling, decisions made by elders and co-operation between different 'tribes'. Gig workers may want to be self-employed but few, if any, want to work alone. Perhaps the traditions of these ancient nomadic tribes should help us to think about what we need from leaders?

Storytellers – Leaders who can create a narrative about the path of the organisation, where it has come from, where it is going, where danger lies and where to go to hunt or gather. (Purpose and Goals)

Decisions made by elders – Leaders who are willing to take responsibility and share their knowledge with others, but who will work as a team to find the right solution for the tribe. (Roles and Rules)

Co-operation between tribes – Leaders who are willing to collaborate with other tribes for the good of the community to help all businesses to survive and grow. (Relationships)

So what does this mean for talent? Perhaps these will be the desired characteristics of leaders of the future. Potentially, the blend of different skills will not be possible to find in one person and so the make-up of the entire 'leadership team' will need to be the focus of a talent review. It will need to pay attention to whether skills of the team complement each other, duplicate or detract. This means that understanding the constituent parts, i.e. who the individual leaders are, will become vital for organisations to ensure that they have a team of winners.

How do we stop leaders from derailing?

Sometimes you can learn more about a subject by looking at what goes wrong. This is how the whole area of derailment has been developed. 'Derailment' is just as it sounds, executives who are on a trajectory to being promoted to the top of organisations but who fail to make it. The cost of failed leadership can be enormous, and as such talent initiatives in organisations rightly attempt to address and halt derailment wherever possible. There are as many theories of derailment as there are of leadership, but a popular and well-researched model is that of the Dark Triad[72], which groups different behaviours into ones in which a leader behaves in a way where they:

- Move Away – try to succeed by intimidation and avoiding others

- Move Against – try to succeed by charm and manipulation

- Move Towards – try to succeed by ingratiating others and building alliances.

For those leaders with a tendency to exhibit these inappropriate behaviours, generally in a situation in which the leader is under pressure or frustrated, this will lead to them being ineffective in organisations. Inevitably this will cost some of them their jobs and may do untold damage to the organisation.

Sometimes the use of a psychometric test or a questionnaire can be incredibly helpful to give a leader and their team the vocabulary to talk about difference in a neutral, non-judgmental context. Using this in a real life business setting will shift learning whilst also delivering business targets. This open dialogue, based around a framework, provides an oasis of calm, where judgment on both sides can be suspended and a proper conversation can be had about how to unblock thinking. Individual assessments based on psychometric tests, such as Hogan Personality Inventory (HPI), Hogan Dark Side (HDS) and Hogan Motives Values Preferences Inventory (MVPI), can be an effective way to surface and address leadership behaviours that help or hinder a leader in their progress.

How do you improve team leadership?

But what happens if the behaviour is specific to a project team, or a team that has been working together for a short time? Individual assessment and coaching can be very powerful, but sometimes team coaching can be helpful to shift unhelpful team dynamics that are threatening to undermine the effectiveness of the leader and the success of the team.

A tool such as Myers Briggs can be used, not to label people, but to help individuals to understand themselves and each other better. It facilitates a conversation about valuing difference. Used in the right way, it helps teams to appreciate and value each other and improves performance.

Example:

Service advisers in a business were consistently receiving feedback from customers that fell short of excellent service. Complaints centred around customers being left waiting, or not being sure when things would happen because they had not had the promised phone call. Customer satisfaction feedback was low and focused on

---

the department not being very friendly. As a result, customers were going elsewhere and not recommending this company to others. Profits were down and the reputation of the business was being compromised.

The team manager called in a team coach to review how to improve the team and work out what could be done to retrieve the situation. Interviews with the team showed up the fact that, although they all liked each other on a social level and had been socialising together, there was a lack of respect for each other. They did not like, or approve of, the way in which other team members worked and found that operating together was confusing. Agreements that had been made about 'team working' did not stick, and some members continued to work in the same way, despite having agreed to change, and this was annoying for other team members.

The team coach used a questionnaire called Myers Briggs Type Indicator (MBTI) on how to identify difference and to value those around you. This had an immediate impact on the team, who recognised the different ways in which they worked as individuals and how this was blocking progress. In the light of this new information about themselves, the team was more able to give each other feedback to ask for support and help in changing. They agreed how to build on the strengths of the team and minimise the weaknesses. Understanding and valuing difference using a framework allowed them to talk about difference in a non-judgmental way. Team operating processes were agreed and put in place.

As a result the team were much happier and more understanding of themselves and the different contributions from each of the team members and the team leader. It helped them to understand the interactions that they had as a team and as individuals with other teams in the company with whom they had to interact. It also helped them to better understand the customer perspective and re-frame the comments being made in a helpful manner.

The team began to work differently. They reported that the atmosphere between them improved and the interactions with the manager got better. Customer complaints fell dramatically and custofner satisfaction rose by 20% over a three-month period. Repeat business began to return and the reputation of the business improved. Finances improved and bonuses began being paid to the team for the first time in 12 months.

Another tool that helps leaders to embed themselves in a new role is a process to accelerate getting to a new leader very quickly. It needs to be facilitated by a third party, preferably a coach. It allows the team to ask questions of the new leader in a safe way so that the trust in the team builds much more quickly, and more importantly the vulnerability demonstrated by leaders can be demonstrated in a controlled way, which allows them to go even deeper. It means that teams can reach a much better understanding of each other and in a way which provides a step change improvement in team performance.

Example:

A team of high-performing scientists were brought together to work on a specific project. The newly-appointed director held a reputation for being a hard taskmaster, formidable and difficult to approach. People didn't know very much about him because he was a very private person. But they knew that he had a reserved nature in meetings, asking critical questions in a way that made most people feel very uncomfortable. Annoyingly for many, he also seemed to be right a great deal of the time.

It was critical to the business that this new project should start to perform at very high levels as fast as possible to beat the competition. There had been rumours flying about the leadership that the team would receive, and a number of key players were unsure about whether they wanted to stay in the team, or be transferred.

The director called in a team coach. The director and coach agreed a plan of action and key deliverables: the team needed to be more open to give and receive feedback and commit to staying on the project. The team coach immediately conducted a series of one-to-one interviews with the team members to answer a set of questions about the director. The answers were then consolidated and anonymised so that there was no way to identify who had said what. Then the team coach met with the director to review the findings the night before a team event. During this discussion the director revealed that he was cripplingly shy and that the way that he approached the team was to disguise this. The coach encouraged the director to talk more about this and they agreed that the best way to counter some of the views held by the team was to disclose this information.

The next day the team coach went through each of the questions and the answers from the team. The director made comments and gave replies. At the appropriate point, where he had some feedback from the team about his style, he revealed that he was shy and what he did to mask it. The atmosphere, which until then had been very tense, immediately changed. The team relaxed and rallied to support the director. The director was able to ask for their help in ensuring that his behaviour did not regress to the 'old' style.

As a result the team was enormously successful. It achieved its targets months ahead of the competition, delivered a revenue boost to the business of millions of dollars, as well as developing some new opportunities for the future. The atmosphere in the team improved beyond recognition and nobody left the team.

Leadership development exercises that focus on team dynamics, can provide great insight for a team where they are co-located but are even more critical in a virtual setting. Social technology has eroded boundaries and so anyone can access Facebook, LinkedIn and Twitter accounts to see what sort of person you are, or have been. This means that organisations who provide these services have become adept at providing software to allow us to do this. Their whole purpose has been to create communities and share knowledge and yet now their most important role is to help "repel all borders". This can limit the formation of teams, so it is even more important for norms and practices to be explicit, practised and understood by all.

Example:

In preparing for a major bid it became clear that the project team, which was full of very senior, highly-experienced people, was working individually rather than together. Feedback from the early stages of the bid process showed that the client was beginning to doubt the members of the team. The client liked the team leader, but was less convinced by other team members. The team were operating as individuals. In presenting to their customer they were using logical, rational, reasoning arguments focused on how the proposal would save the client money which is what appealed to them. However, it was evident that the customer was not working from this basis, but was more influenced by what would happen to their people. The team leader was also influencing on this basis but was not able to convince his team members that they needed to adapt their own styles which had always been very successful for them in the past.

The team leader called in a team coach, who after the initial interviews designed an intervention to look at how the team could elevate itself to high-performance team working by adopting co-coaching and collaborative team working.

The coach used a combination of models: Firo-B, a test designed by Will Schutz who used it to identify superior team working in the US Navy on warships, together with Myers Briggs. This illustrated how the team needed to behave differently with the client who was more likely to be swayed by emotional, values-based logic. Once this was clear, then the team could proceed with the bid ensuring that the wording in the proposal and presentation properly reflected the concerns of the customer.

Firo-B opened up the team to being really open and honest with each other, in a way that they had simply not been doing previously. This changed the dynamic and the team started to coach one another, highly successfully, and remind each other when written work or presentations fell short of what the customer would want to hear.

As a result of this intervention, a £40m piece of work was won. It was agreed that all bid teams would go through this analysis, and that the wording of any customer-facing literature would be reviewed in the light of ensuring that it properly reflected the customer's preferences, rather than those of the bid team. The team members continued to coach each other and were successful in winning other bids.

The shift in business models that has been created by the gig economy and globalisation can add an extra dimension to leadership that some leaders may never have encountered. Leading an international team may create a steep learning curve for leaders as they try to apply what has worked for them in the past. If they are to progress in their careers, they will need to unlearn what they know and adopt a new set of knowledge skills and behaviours, preferably in a smaller assignment, where collateral damage is more limited and can be managed appropriately. A project or small assignment can provide valuable learning.

Example:

A project group with a variety of different Europeans was set up to consider a strategic marketing issue for the Italian business. The project was deliberately set up to deliver tangible business results, but also to maximise learning, so a coach was appointed to each mixed nationality team. The project was being run by a German team leader, and when he wasn't around an Austrian took over. The meetings started at 9am and ran until 10am via Skype. On each occasion the Italian and Spanish team members were late. This began to cause tension in the team.

It became apparent through the intervention of the coach that the Italians and Spanish all worked until much later in the evening, but started much later in the day. So they were equally fed up with the team because they were feeling that they were having pressure put on them to arrive earlier than they would normally need to. They would normally start work at 11am and felt that they were making extra effort to be there earlier. Once this was clear, the team leader moved the meeting to midday and the tension in the team disappeared.

Simple steps such as this provided valuable insight for the young leaders involved into how to avoid making assumptions about people you are leading and ensured that the project delivered on time and budget.

In summary, it would be an understatement to say that leadership is difficult. It is hard to define, and done well, or badly, has a huge impact on the success or otherwise of an organisation. Reams of articles and thousands of books have been written on the subject, probably because it is such a challenge and everyone has something to say about leaders they have known and loved and those they have hated, in equal measure.

The job of Talent is to facilitate the finding, growing and keeping of leaders who are going to be the most beneficial for their organisation. In this chapter I have attempted to synthesise down the vast amount of literature into some small, practical steps that organisations might consider in figuring it out for themselves. This is by no means intended to be a panacea or a complete guide to what is a very complex subject, but is rather more of a starting point for an organisation to begin thinking about what they really want from their leaders.

Top Tips:

+ Understand what you want from your leaders.

+ Review and incorporate the ways in which leadership
  is changing both now and in the future. E.g. Invest in
  storytelling, collective decision making and collaboration.

+ Recognise the impact that Corporate Nomads are having on
  how leaders need to lead, and work this into a framework.

+ Help leaders to see themselves as others see them and work
  on the factors that may derail them before that happens.

+ Coach teams as well as individual leaders and provide insight
  into how team dynamics can help or hinder team success.

CHAPTER 12

CONCLUSION

The business of finding, growing and keeping the right people in your organisation gets harder on a daily basis, as the concept of what that organisation actually is and how it operates is being continuously challenged. What this means for the talent agenda is that it needs to be at the heart of business strategy to ensure that the organisation has the right type and right amount of people that it needs to achieve its aims, both now and in the future.

Research has shown that whilst businesses and the wider economy are changing rapidly, people are not. What attracts them to an organisation, how they are developed and what will motivate them may be subtly evolving but in essence human behaviour is not changing all that much. Evidence from research shows that what is important to people is how they are led and managed, and so leaders can be reassured that they can still impact people by using many of the same leadership qualities that they have been honing for years. What may need to change is the approach and practices of talent management to ensure that it keeps pace with the ambitions of the organisation.

Talent management is essentially about managing risk. This has traditionally been easier to do in larger organisations where the pace of change has been slower, but with the changes in the economy, as well as changes in technology, the business of talent needs to reinvent itself and consider how effective it can be in the future. Across all businesses. Even in those large enterprises that have not changed for decades progress is pushing them along.

Many of the current practices in talent management are sound and still have a place in business. But in a society where information is freely available, trends and ideas are being publicised which are lacking the rigour of research to back them up. Large businesses with dedicated teams can take the time to read into the ideas and construct ways of operating that are effective. But in smaller businesses, where they do not have the luxury of spending time determining what to do, there is a temptation to simply go with the headline and, for example, 'get rid of appraisals', instead of standing back and improving what is already there. This book offers an alternative interpretation of some of the trends and makes a case for some sound practices that will benefit any organisation.

In finding talent the key will be for organisations to be really clear about what they want and need, both now and in the future. A certain amount of agility and creativeness is required to ensure that the supply and demand is constant. This means that those parts of the organisation charged with finding the right people need to be abreast of what is happening or is going to happen in the business, if they are to be effective. The starting point is to be really clear about the problem you are trying to solve, and ensure that everyone involved is bought in. Understanding and keeping up to date with changes in the business model and altering talent processes accordingly is critical. An outsourced model will create different needs in the business. The talent agenda can both support and challenge new business models, such as the gig economy. Linking together talent selection, talent development and talent retention through the processes that are used will help organisations to operationalise their people strategy effectively and efficiently.

Introducing Strategic Resource Planning that captures not only current but also future needs is key. Using talent reviews to consider key roles, as well as the core commonly-considered leadership roles, will help to manage risk for an organisation. Risks in key technical roles can be just as, if not more, damaging to a business if they are not identified and addressed in time. It can be helpful to use customers, talent pool members and external experts to help scenario plan 'what ifs' to encourage the development of new roles that may be completely novel. Using current and future talent pools to challenge the status quo through development initiatives and programmes can be a useful exercise in engaging them, and will also provide fresh insight to the future challenges of the organisation.

Implementation of the talent agenda needs leadership from the top of the organisation for it to be truly successful. Managers may need support to understand and execute their role in talent and embrace all aspects of the talent agenda; training, support, challenge and clear guidelines on what their role is will all help to set them up for success.

Careful consideration of the focus of the talent agenda will help you to make an informed decision about whether it should have open or closed membership. Implications for both should be discussed and consequences for managing it understood by all. This decision should be linked to the values of the business. Making membership optional and flexible, so that members can accommodate the needs of their personal lives, will ensure that it does not discriminate. Every leader and manager needs to understand what 'performance' and 'potential' mean in their organisation and ensure that they do not apply definitions from previous places where they have worked. They need to manage risk carefully, avoiding being over dependent on one or two key candidates who are successors for multiple roles, but not able to fill all of them; take a risk and help forecast needs in a way that allows under-represented groups to be eligible for roles.

In growing talent the CEO is key to success. Demonstrating their commitment to both the programme and to their own learning, by telling others about it, or role modelling by attending programmes, will be a powerful incentive to make sure that people are taking their own development seriously.

In growing talent they need to recognise that technology has changed the language of new generations coming through, but not assume that technology is the answer to training future generations. It may be one answer, but the jury is out on its effectiveness in its current format.

Keeping talent is complex. Motivation is not necessarily changing, but essentially there is no evidence to suggest that millennials differ in what they want from the workplace. So do not be tempted to treat them any differently. People are motivated by goals, feedback and comparing themselves to others, so SMART is still a really good tool to use, and getting rid of appraisals makes no sense. It would be better to review what you currently do and improve that through training and revising the process. Not having a performance rating will impact how you manage the talent assessment process.

Businesses need to challenge themselves to think differently about their employees and what they want from work. They need to be doing this on a regular basis. Understanding what 'talent' wants is part of an ongoing regular dialogue. Holding regular meetings to discuss career aspirations will help.

Reconsidering the talent agenda in the light of changing employment and labour forces is an important debate to be having now. The rise of non-traditional careers, the gig economy and what that means for a business need to be explored at a market and organisational level. Businesses may need to re-think how they engage with those outside the confines of their own businesses. Introducing returners' engagement programmes are a great way to bring key players back into the workforce. Supporting non-traditional careers through the psychological contract and other ways will give companies the edge in attracting key talent back into the workplace. Providing outreach programmes and seeing less rigid boundaries between the workplace and other employers will be critical to survival. Lobbying government to challenge the traditional employment contract will be important to determine how far a business can go in providing support. Businesses need to be able to grow and reshape to meet market forces. Talent is one way to structure that business development and ensure that it is able to deliver.

Leadership deserves a special mention because of the scale of the impact it can have on the success, or otherwise, of an organisation. It is hard to define and so it is hard to find, grow and keep the right leaders in your organisation. And yet there are some core principles that remain. Leaders need to be able to innovate, inspire, support, role model and encourage their followers. In the new gig economy they may need to think about how they take 'Corporate Nomads' with them on the journey, maybe learning the lessons of storytelling, collective decision making and collaboration with other 'tribes'. Organisations that help leaders to understand their 'dark side' and avoid them derailing will be adding to the well-being of the leader as well as their followers. Learning to understand team dynamics is going to be increasingly important as organisations become more diffuse.

In summary, talent is a key organisational tool that when used well can add to the development and success of an organisation. It encompasses a number of different activities, and when aligned and working well has the ability to enhance productivity, increase well-being and boost share price. Talent needs to keep pace with changes happening in society and in business so that it can stay relevant and support organisational goals. It has to be reviewed and amended on a continuous basis to reflect the 'new normal'. The only question I have left is, 'Why wouldn't you use it?'

APPENDIX

TALENT HEALTH AUDIT

Company Name:

1. What works in our talent initiatives?

2. What doesn't work?

3. How important are the following to the business?

   On a scale of (least important) 1 – 10 (most important)

   a. Find Talent

   b. Grow Talent

   c. Keep Talent

4. How effective are the following in our business?

   On a scale of (least important) 1 – 10 (most important)

   a. Find Talent

   b. Grow Talent

   c. Keep Talent

5. What's the one thing that we need to improve? Why?

   Now ask yourself these questions again and find out what the rest of the business thinks.

   Do managers and employees agree?

   What criteria are you applying?

   What evidence do you have for giving these ratings?

ENDNOTE REFERENCES

Chapter 2

1   'The Boundaryless Career: A new perspective for organisational Inquiry', Arthur, M., Journal of Organizational Behavior Volume 15, Issue 4, July 1994, pp 295-306.

2   'The New Career Contract: Developing the Whole Person at Midlife and Beyond', Hall, DT. Journal of Vocational Behavior, Volume 47, Issue 3, December 1995, pp 269-289.

3   'IBM was a pioneer in the work-from-home revolution – now it's cracking down', Article in Business Insider UK, Chris Weller, 18 May 2017.

4   Guest, David E., HRM and the Worker: Towards a New Psychological Contract? In: Boxall, Peter (Editor); Purcell, John (Editor); Wright, Patrick (Editor). Oxford Handbook of Human Resource Management, Oxford University Press, 2007: pp 128-146.

Chapter 3

5   *The Innovators Dilemma*, Clayton Christensen 1997.

6   *6 Thinking Hats*, Edward De Bono, 1985.

7   Exploring the value of an O*NET resource for the UK', Report from a workshop held in London, June 2015. Jim Hillage, Michael Cross.

Chapter 4

8   Lau, D. C., & Murnighan, J. K. (2005). 'Interactions within Groups and Subgroups: The Effects of Demographic Faultlines', The Academy of Management Journal, 48(4), pp 645-659.

9   Herring, C. (2009). Does Diversity Pay?: Race, Gender, and the Business Case for Diversity', American Sociological Review, 74(2), pp 208-224.

10   Women and Leadership. Public Says Women are Equally Qualified, but Barriers Persist', January 14, 2015. Pew Institute.Wharton University

11   Di Tomaso, N., Post, C., & Parks-Yancy, R. (2007). Workforce Diversity and Inequality: Power, Status, and Numbers', Annual Review of Sociology, 33, pp 473-501.

12   Blake-Davis, A., Broschak, J., P. & George, E. (2003). Happy Together? How using non-standard workers affects exit, voice and loyalty among standard employees', Academy of Management Journal, 46(4), pp 475-485.

Broschak, J., P., & Davis-Blake, A. (2006). 'Mixing Standard work and non-standard deals: the consequences of heterogeneity in employment relationships', Academy of Management Journal, 49(2), pp 371-393.

Chapter 5

13   Millennials at work. Reshaping the Workplace, 2011, 2014, PwC.

14   What Do Millennials Really Want at Work? The Same Things the Rest of Us Do. Bruce N. Pfau, April 2016.

15   'Generational Differences in Work-Related Attitudes: A Meta-analysis', David P. Costanza, Jessica M. Badger, Rebecca L. Fraser, Jamie B. Severt and Paul A. Gade. Journal of Business and Psychology. Vol. 27, No. 4 (December 2012), pp 375-394.

16   'Myths, Exaggerations and Uncomfortable Truths: The Real Story Behind Millennials in the Workplace', IBM Institute for Business Value, 2015.

17   'Can Conflicting Perspectives on the Role of g in Personnel Selection Be Resolved?', Kevin R. Murphy, Human Performance, 15(1/2), pp 173-186 2002.

Chapter 6

18   Janeelliott.com

Chapter 7

19   Assessment Center Dimensions: Individual differences correlates and meta-analytic incremental validity, Dilchert & Ones, International Journal of Selection and Assessment, Volume 17, Issue 3, September 2009 pp 254-270.

20   Schmidt, F. L., & Hunter, J. E. (1998). 'The validity and utility of selection methods in personnel psychology: Practical and theoretical implications of 85 years of research findings', *Psychological Bulletin, 124*(2), pp 262-274.

21   Cascio, W. F., & Silbey, V. (1979). Utility of the assessment center as a selection device. Journal of Applied Psychology, 64(2), pp 107-118.

22   Dewberry, Chris and Jordan, Deborah (2006). 'Do consensus meetings undermine the validity of assessment centres?', Division of Occupational Psychology Annual Conference, 11-13 January 2006, Glasgow.

Chapter 8

23   'Why Leadership Development Programs Fail', Pierre Gurdjian, Thomas Halbeisen, and Kevin Lane, McKinsey Quarterly, January 2014.

24   '70:20:10 Where is the Evidence?', Association for Talent Development, 08 July 2014, Andrew Jefferson, Roy Pollock.

25   *Lessons of Experience: How Successful Executives Develop on the Job*, Morgan W. McCall, Michael M. Lombardo, Ann M. Morrison 1998, The Free Press, Lexington Books.

26   'The career architect development planner: a systematic approach to development including 103 research-based and experience-tested development plans and coaching tips : for learners, managers, mentors, and feedback givers', 1996 Lominger Press.

27   Kajewski and Madsen (2012) 'Demystifying 70:20:10' Deakin Prime.

28   'Developing global executives: The lessons of international experience', McCall, GP Hollenbeck - 2002 -Harvard Business Press.

29   'Fail fast, fail often: How losing can help you win', R Babineaux, JD Krumboltz - 2013

30   Marc Prensky, (2001) 'Digital Natives, Digital Immigrants Part 1', On the Horizon, Vol. 9 Issue: 5, pp 1-6.

31   'The Net Generation and Digital Natives Implications for Higher Education', a literature review commissioned by the Higher Education Academy, Dr Christopher Jones and Ms Binhui Shao. The Open University, 26th June 2011.

32   'Are digital natives a myth or reality? University students' use of digital technologies', Anoush Margaryan Allison Littlejohn Gabrielle Vojt Computers & Education, Volume 56, Issue 2, February 2011, pp 429-440.

33   'Evaluating training programs', D.L. Kirkpatrick - 1975 - Tata McGraw-Hill Education.

34   Baldwin, T.T., & Ford, J.K. 1988. 'Transfer of training: A review and directions for future research', Personnel Psychology, 41: pp 63-105.

Chapter 9

35   'Is the job satisfaction–job performance relationship spurious? A meta-analytic examination', Journal of Vocational Behavior Volume 71, Issue 2, October 2007, pp 167-185.

36   'Work & Motivation', VH Vroom - NY: John Wiley & Sons, 1964.

Porter, L. W., & Lawler, E. E. (1965). 'Properties of organization structure in relation to job attitudes and job behavior', *Psychological Bulletin, 64*(1), pp 23-51.

37   Donovan, John J. 'Work motivation', *Handbook of industrial, work and organizational psychology* 2 (2001): pp 53-76.

38   'Equity Theory Revisited: Comments and Annotated Bibliography', J. Stacy Adams, Sara Freedman Advances in Experimental Social Psychology Volume 9, 1976, pp 43-90.

39   Lee, T. W., Locke, E. A., & Latham, G. P. (1989). 'Goal setting theory and job performance', in L. A. Pervin (Ed.), *Goal concepts in personality and social psychology* (pp. 291-326). Hillsdale, NJ: Lawrence Erlbaum Associates.

40   Tubbs, M. E. (1986). 'Goal setting: A meta-analytic examination of the empirical evidence', Journal of Applied Psychology, 71(3), pp 474-483.

41   Latham, G. P., & Baldes, J. J. (1975). 'The "practical significance" of Locke's theory of goal setting', Journal of Applied Psychology, 60(1), pp 122-124.

42   'The Effects of Goal Setting, External Feedback, and Self-Generated Feedback on Outcome Variables: A Field Experiment', John M. Ivancevich and J. Timothy McMahon Academy of Management Journal June 1, 1982 vol. 25 no. 2 pp 359-372 Ludwig, T. D. and Goomas, D. T. (2009), Real-time performance monitoring, goal-setting, and feedback for forklift drivers in a distribution centre. Journal of Occupational and Organizational Psychology, 82: pp 391-403.

43   Erez, M., & Zidon, I. (1984). 'Effect of goal acceptance on the relationship of goal difficulty to performance', Journal of Applied Psychology, 69(1), pp 69-78.

44   Yukl, G. A., and Latham, G. P. (1978), 'Interrelationships among employee participation, individual differences, goal difficulty, goal acceptance, goal instrumentality, and performance', Personnel Psychology, 31: pp 305-323.

45   'Dynamic spread of happiness in a large social network: longitudinal analysis over 20 years in the Framingham Heart Study', BMJ 2008; 337:a2338.

46   Turban D.B., & Keon T.L., Organizational Attractiveness: An Interactionist Perspective (1993) Journal of Applied Psychology Vol. 78. No. 2, pp 184-193.

47   'Dynamic spread of happiness in a large social network: longitudinal analysis over 20 years in the Framingham Heart Study', BMJ 2008; 337:a2338.

48   'The "What" and "Why" of Goal Pursuits: Human Needs and the Self-Determination of Behavior', Edward L. Deci and Richard M. Ryan Psychological Inquiry 2 2000, Vol. 11.

49   'Self-determination theory and work motivation', Marylene Gagne and Edward L. Dec 12; Journal of Organizational Behavior 26, pp 331-362 (2005).

50   'Intrinsic and Extrinsic Motivation. The Review of Economic Studies', 70(3), pp 489-520. Deci, E. L., & Ryan, R. M. (1985). Intrinsic Motivation and Self-Determination in Human Behavior. New York: Plenum Press.; E. L. Deci.

51   Lepper, M. R., & Greene, D. (1975). 'When Two Rewards Are Worse than One: Effects of Extrinsic Rewards on Intrinsic Motivation', The Phi Delta Kappan, 56(8), pp 565-566.

52   Garaus, C., Furtmuller, G., & Guttel, W. G. (2016). The hidden power of small rewards: The effects of insufficient external rewards on autonomous motivation to learn. Academy of Management Learning and Education, 15(1), pp 45-58.

53   Unrau, N., & Schlackman, J. (2006). 'Motivation and its relationship with reading achievement in an urban middle school', The Journal of Educational Research, 100(2), pp 81-101.

54   Robinson, L. J., Stevens, L. H., Threapleton, C. J. D., Vainiute, J., McAllister-Williams, R. H., & Gallagher, P. (2012). 'Effects of intrinsic and extrinsic motivation on attention and memory', Acta Psychologica, 141(2), pp 243-249.

Chapter 10

55   Gerber, M., Grote, G., Geiser, C., & Raeder, S. (2012). 'Managing psychological contracts in the era of the "new" career', [Article]. European Journal of Work and Organisational Psychology, 21(2), pp 195-221.

56   Hall, D. T. (1996). 'Protean Careers of the 21st Century', The Academy of Management Executive (1993-2005), 10(4), pp 8-16.

57   Fontinha, R., Chambel, M. J., & De Cuyper, N. (2014). 'Training and the Commitment of Outsourced Information Technologies' Workers: Psychological Contract Fulfillment as a Mediator', [Article]. Journal of Career Development, 41(4), pp 321-340.

58   Ituma, A., & Simpson, R. (2009). 'The 'boundaryless' career and career boundaries: Applying an institutionalist perspective to ICT workers in the context of Nigeria', [10.1177/0018726709103456]. Human Relations, 62(5), pp 727-761.

59   Cao, L., Hirschi, A., & Deller, J. (2011). 'Self-initiated expatriates and their career success', The Journal of management development, 31(2), pp 159-172.

60   Hess, N., Jepsen, D. M., & Dries, N. (2012). 'Career and employer change in the age of the 'boundaryless' career', Journal of Vocational Behavior, 81(2), pp 280-288.

Martin, G., John, A., & Crispin, C. (2014). 'Organisational boundaries and beyond: A new look at the components of a boundaryless career orientation', Career Development International, 19(6), pp 641-667.

61   Arthur, M. B. (2014). 'The boundaryless career at 20: where do we stand, and where can we go?', Career Development International, 19(6), pp 627-640.

62   Haynie, J. M., & Shepherd, D. (2011). 'Toward a Theory of Discontinuous Career Transition: Investigating Career Transitions Necessitated by Traumatic Life Events', Journal of Applied Psychology, 96(3), pp 501-524.

63   Savickas, M., L., (2012). 'Life Design: A paradigm for career intervention in the 21st Century', Journal of Counseling and Development, 90, pp 13-17.

64   Ladge, J. J., Clair, J. A., & Greenburg, D. (2012). 'Cross-Domain Identity Transition During Liminal Periods: Constructing multiple selves as professional and mother during pregnancy', Academy of Management Journal, 55(6), pp 1449-1471.

65   Super, D. E. (1957). 'Vocational development: a framework for research', New York, USA: Teachers College, Columbia University.

66   Lee, M. D., Kossek, E. E., Hall, D., T, & Litricio, J.-B. (2011). 'Entangled strands: A process perspective on the evolution of careers in the context of personal, family, work and community life', Human Relations, 64(12), pp 1531-1553.

67   Mainiero, L. A., & Sullivan, S. E. (2005). 'Kaleidoscope careers: An alternate explanation for the "opt-out" revolution', Academy of Management Executive, 19(106-123).

68   Clarek, M. (2015). 'Dual Careers: The new norm for Gen Y Professionals?' Career Development International, 20(6), pp 562-582.

Chapter 11

69   '2020 Vision: future trends in leadership and management', ILM 2014.

70   'Development and Validation of the Leadership Practices Inventory', Barry Z. Posner, Educational and Psychological Measurement Vol 48, Issue 2, pp 483-496, First published: September 7 2016.

71   'Nomadic Culture: Cultural Support for Working Anytime, Anywhere', *Leida Chen & Ravi Nath,* Information Systems Management Vol. 22, Iss. 4, 2005.

72   Hogan, J., Hogan, R., & Kaiser, R. B. (2010). 'Management derailment', *APA handbook of industrial and organizational psychology, 3,* pp 555-575.

ABOUT THE AUTHOR

Kate O'Loughlin is an executive coach and HR consultant, specialising in Talent Management. She is married to Chris and they live in a falling-down thatched cottage in Wiltshire. Kate is passionate about helping people get the most out of organisations and what leaders need to do to make that happen. She has worked with a wide variety of people from chief executives to graduates, in organisations large, small and medium sized, both international and local.

26752606R00090

Printed in Great Britain
by Amazon